GUERNSEY
AS IT USED TO BE

A Tour of the Town in Victorian Times

BY

GEORGE W.J.L HUGO

with an introduction and index
by Stephen Foote

BLUE
ORMER

MMXVII

Published in 2017 by Blue Ormer Publishing

www.blueormer.co.uk

Main text copyright © George William Joseph Lewis Hugo, 1933.

Introduction and Index copyright © Stephen Foote, 2017.

All illustrations, except where otherwise stated, are from the Priaulx Library collections, and are reproduced with their permission.

Cover Design by Edward Bettison.

Printed by Short Run Press, Exeter.

ISBN: 978-0-9928791-2-9

CONTENTS

Introduction 5

Paved Streets 11

Smith Street 13

High Street 17

The Pollet 23

The Commercial Arcade & Market Street 27

Fountain Street & Le Bordage 37

Mill Street & Mansell Street 43

Trinity Square & Vauvert Road 49

The Borders of the Town 53

General Topics 59

Amusements 63

Miscellaneous 69

The Bathing Places 79

The Tramway 81

Newspapers 83

Ships & Harbour 85

Map of St Peter Port 94

List of Illustrations 96

Index 98

George William Joseph Lewis Hugo (1862-1936)

INTRODUCTION

Although many of the online genealogy services would have you believe that you can quite quickly trace your family tree back a century or more with a few clicks on their website, the resulting list of names and dates can often leave you wondering who these people were, what they were like and how they spent their time.

This was George Hugo's intention when he wrote this book in the 1930s. He began his original introduction:

> I make no pretence of having, in the following few pages, written an exhaustive social history of Guernsey. My narrative is but the outcome of a wish expressed by members of my family that I would leave them some account of things that are no more and of people who have passed away.[1]

George Hugo was born in St Peter Port in 1862, the same year that the Bathing Places opened at La Valette. So the period he is describing is largely from his first memories around the late 1860s until the birth of his younger children in the early 20th century.

It was a time when getting around the island was much more difficult than it is now. St Julian's Avenue and the Val des Terres had yet to be built – so the main routes in and out of town were the narrow and hilly cobbled streets such as Smith Street and Cornet Street – both of which were narrower than they are today. Since horse-drawn carriages, or walking, were the only modes of transport, the rest of the island must have seemed rather remote – certainly many of the author's recollections are centred around the people and places in St Peter Port.

The Town's shops were largely family-run affairs, with none of the national retailers that we are familiar with today. However, there are a surprising number of businesses mentioned in this account that will be familiar from today's town centre: Beghin's, Bucktrout's, Creasey's, A.P Roger, and Machon's, as well as the not-too-distant-memories of stores such as Le Riche's, Grut's, Best Butchers, and Fuzzey's.

---

1   G.W.J.L. Hugo, *Guernsey As It Used To Be: Some Aspects of the Island in my Boyhood, Youth and Early Manhood with Allusions to Well-Known Persons* (Guernsey Star & Gazette, 1933).

Islanders had far less leisure time, and less to do with the little free time they had. Some of these activities are still popular today, such as excursions to Herm and Sark – others, such as meeting the boat from England or attending the regimental band performance at Cambridge Park, have largely disappeared from the social calendar.

At this time, horticultural exports (particularly grapes and tomatoes) were overtaking shipbuilding and the export of granite as the mainstay of the island's economy. You can tell that the tourist industry was still in its infancy, as Mr. Hugo recalls his surprise at counting as many as twenty-two visiting yachts in the harbour.

The result is a fascinating account of Guernsey as it was during the Victorian period, brought to life with stories of the Town's characters and how they spent their time. It captures the way of life in the islands at a time before the dramatic effects of two world wars, the sweeping technical advances of the 20th century and the rise of the finance industry.

With the exception of this introduction, what follows is the author's original text, including footnotes. For the benefit of those interested in particular people, businesses or other aspects of the island during this period, a comprehensive index has been compiled.

About the Author

Considering this work was originally intended primarily for his family, it is maybe not surprising that it includes little in the way of personal details about the author himself. He must have assumed that they already knew all about him.

Despite his familiar surname, the family were not related to their French namesake, Victor Hugo – the most famous resident of St Peter Port at that time – although the author does admit to having met him.

George William Joseph Lewis Hugo was born in Guernsey in 1862, the

1867 Guernsey Almanack

son of Samuel George Hugo and Ellen (née Fielder). George's grandfather, Samuel, was originally from Feock in Cornwall but left there when his speculation in mining ventures resulted in the loss of the family fortune. He spent three years in Exeter training to be a dentist and moved to Guernsey in August 1841 with his family for a fresh start. He trained all three of his sons in dental surgery. The two eldest moved to Jersey and set up practice there. His third son, Samuel George, continued his father's practice at 15 Allez Street, St Peter Port until his death in 1912.

The Hugos were at the forefront of developments in dentistry in the island. In January 1847, *The Star* newspaper reported that Samuel Hugo was the first dentist to use ether as an anaesthetic – in fact, it was just a few weeks after it had first been successfully used anywhere in Europe.[2] By the 1870s dental surgery was becoming established as a profession, with fillings, reclining chairs and anaesthetics all part of the dentist's armoury, and in 1878, the British Parliament had passed the Dentists Act which limited the use of the title Dentist to those who were suitably qualified.[3] Although it would be another ten years before the States of Guernsey introduced the equivalent regulations,[4] Samuel and his son, George, were among the first dentists inscribed on the British Dentists' Register.[5]

In 1891, George married Marie-Madeleine Guérin, at St. Joseph's Church in Guernsey. Madeleine was the daughter of Jules-Prosper Guérin of St. Hilaire-du-Harcouët in Normandy. George dedicated the book: 'to my wife who, though not a Guernseywoman, is enamoured of the island and of its people'.

Together they raised a family of ten children. However, by the time Hugo wrote this memoir in 1933, four of his seven sons had passed away and two of his three daughters had married and left the island.[6] His youngest son, Tom, remained in Guernsey – and his descendants are still living in the

---

2   'Painless Operations', *The Star*, 22 January 1847. Quoted in Bernhard Panning, 'Early Reports of the Introduction of Ether as an Anaesthetic Agent in the Guernsey newspapers', *Transactions of La Societe Guernesiaise*, XXVI:4 (2009).

3   British Dental Association Museum website, www.bda.org/museum.

4   'Ordonnance par rapport aux Dentistes', *Receuil d'Ordonnances de la Cour Royale de L'Ile de Guernesey*, ed. Arthur Bell, Vol IV (1900), p.347.

5   Correspondence with British Dental Association Museum, 2016.

6   A more detailed account of the Hugo family's history can be found in a booklet written by George's son, Francis H.M. Hugo, *A Pedigree of the Family of Hugo of St. Feock, Cornwall*, printed by Frederick Clarke for private circulation in 1932. A copy can be found in the Priaulx Library, Guernsey.

island today.

Whilst there are few personal references in this memoir, there is one comment which deserves a little explanation, due to the author's modesty. On page 69, there is a passing reference to a fire in Allez Street. According to the newspaper account it was a devastating blaze, which destroyed three adjacent houses in the street and rendered four families homeless. The fire started in the early hours of the morning of 30 April 1887, and whilst the fire engine was quickly on the scene, the nearest public water tank had just been cleaned and was empty. With no running water, the fire fighters were dependent on members of the public ferrying buckets of water back and forth to fill the tank of the fire engine. After a local business provided access to their water tank, the fire was eventually extinguished thanks to the help of a number of members of the public – amongst those singled out for praise in the newspaper's report was Mr. George Hugo.[7]

George Hugo died in 1936, a little over two years after the book was published. His obituary in *The Star*, claimed:

> Mr Hugo was of a charming disposition which had endeared him to a large circle of friends and acquaintances. It may be remembered that he published about two years ago a charming little book which was entitled *Guernsey as it used to be* in which he gave a graphic description of the changes he had seen in the town since he was a boy.[8]

Acknowledgements

I am very grateful to Sue Laker and Becky Nel at the Priaulx Library in Guernsey, who have provided invaluable assistance in seeking out illustrations from the library's collections to accompany the text, partially inspired by their 2015 exhibition *How Guernsey Used to Shop*.

I would also like to thank: Peter Hugo, the author's grandson, for providing information on his family's history, as well as the family photographs which appear on pages 4 & 9; the British Dental Association Museum, for information on the professional careers of Samuel and George Hugo; Lisa Burton of the Guernsey Museum for permission to reproduce the photograph of Marmain's Stores on page 46; the Royal Court for their kind permission to reproduce the portrait of Sir Peter Stafford Carey on page 61 and Edward Bettison for his excellent cover design.

Stephen Foote, February 2017.

---

7 'Serious Fire: Four Families Burnt Out', *The Star*, Guernsey, 30 April 1887.

8 'Funeral of Mr George Hugo', *The Star*, Guernsey, 16 January 1936.

George & Marie-Madeleine Hugo and family, 1906.

Clockwise from top: George, Miriam, Edward, Helen, George junior (seated), Marie-Madeleine (wife) with baby Francis, Bernard, Catherine, Cyril.

Family outing to Petit Bot, 1920s. George Hugo second from left.

Cobbled Street: corner of Fountain Street and Church Hill, opposite Town Church

PAVED STREETS

One of the earliest of my memories and keenest of my regrets is the pavement of our streets. McAdam may have been a benefactor(?), but I wish he'd been John Stone. In those days of iron tyres, the noise, of course, was very great, so that you could hardly hear a secret told you in the open, but we had iron nerves to match and were happy in the wonderful cleanliness of our town and in the ease with which we kept dirt from our doors. Scrapers, as we know them now, were not in common use. Most houses had a small recess on one side of the doorway with a broad blade of iron fixed across it. In the more important dwellings, an elaborate arrangement stood at each side of the entrance. Ah! Had I thought of it in time, I might have asked for one of those blue granite setts as a relic of past days. It would have made a splendid paper weight, or would have done to keep a door open!

Smith Street (Rue des Forges) was, I think, the first to go. It was the most irregular of all our thoroughfares and needed alteration. Besides being uneven, the pavement there was much more worn than in the other streets, Quay Street, perhaps, excepted. Coupled with its steep ascent, it made it difficult for horses. St. James's Street (Profonde Rue) and the Grange received attention later, and then a pause was made for several years, Sausmarez Street, St. John Street, Havilland Street, Union Street, and Allez Street – all comprised in "New Town" – remaining paved long after. Le Bordage was among the last, it seems to me, to be macadamized. Patent Victoria Stone replaced the broad stone flags of the Arcade and appears to do as well.

Smith Street

SMITH STREET

In Smith Street have taken place the greatest changes that I remember. At the bottom on the right as one looked up the street, there stood a house in which, I think, there was a bakery. A few smaller houses followed in a zigzag fashion, that in which Mr. Field, bootmaker, pursued his calling, looking downward. A large one higher up was Mrs. Durant's, and there she kept a toyshop. The entrance to the house was curious. The door divided in two halves, a lower and an upper one like that of some farmhouses, opened on a few stone steps which, turning once, descended to the passage with the toyshop on the right. I remember the old lady well, her wares naturally attracting me in boyhood. Perhaps a little under middle height, she was yet broad and plump, her hair, as was a custom at the time, being confined in a net behind her head and, I think, a band of black velvet tied in a bow passed over it. In an apartment opposite the toyshop, Mrs. Le Lacheur, her widowed daughter, started the successful baby linen business. She continued when alterations to Smith Street were in progress and the old house was demolished across the way and, later, carried on by Mrs. G. Wheadon and her daughters.

Above Mrs. Durant's house, the street receded many feet, forming a paved yard in front of some smaller dwellings, in one of which Mrs. Brennan, grocer, tea dealer, etc., and Miss Duplain, umbrella repairer, did business. As far as I remember, a garden wall extended from these houses to that used for so many years by Mr. Charles Kitts as an office and which I'm told was once the town house of the de Sausmarez family of St. Martins. When, later, shops were built, Mr. B. Collenette photographer, took one of

Hartwell's Piano store, Smith Street

them, while Mr. J. Shaw, paperhanger and decorator, succeeded in business by Mr. Paul Whinfield, occupied the one next door.

The Post Office in Nelson Place was built a short time afterwards and was owned by Mr. Shaw, whose heirs probably retain possession.

On the other side of Smith Street, but further up than Mr. Kitts', was Mrs. Angel, bookseller. As Miss M.A. Barbet, Mrs. Angel, sister to Mr. Stephen Barbet, had, I think, commenced this business before her marriage. She died but recently, at the house of her son-in-law, Mr. Martin, in Candie Road, having, a month or so before, completed her hundredth year. After a short occupation by another bookseller, the business became "Gaudin's". The house, like that next door below, was double-fronted. On the left of the passage entering Mrs. Angel's, Mr. J. B. Torode, écrivain, and his son after him, had offices. Messrs. P. Le Page and Son, watch and clockmakers, occupied the shop in the adjoining house, Mr. Le Page, jun., moving, I think, after many years, into what had been Messrs. Torodes' premises. The shops have since been sub-divided.

The present office[1] of the Guernsey Gaslight Company was once a large dwelling house, but was transformed some sixty years ago for Messrs.

---

1   Undergoing (June-Aug., 1933) still further modification, the Gaslight Co. having acquired the house next door above.

14

Hartwell and Woodward's piano business. It was, if I am not deceived, the earliest attempt in town at a more modern kind of shop and at the time was considered somewhat venturesome. The open space beside it with the flight of steps existed then, but in a rough condition.

On the site of Mrs. Wheadon's, or quite near, there stood an ancient house and shop in which, as a boy, I have watched Mr. H. Turner, bookbinder, at work, shaving the edges of his volumes. This was separated by a wall from a few others lower down. One, I know, was raised above the street and, though small, was double-fronted. A few steps were in the doorway. Berlin wool, tatting needles, cotton and the like, as well as fancy needlework, were sold there by two elderly ladies[2] whose names I have forgotten, though I remember well the portly build and corkscrew curls of one of them. At one time, Mr. Gray, hairdresser, occupied another of these shops. Mr. Philpot's chemist's shop was the last one in the street. The business was taken over afterwards by Mr. Harold. In 1877 or 1878, Mr. Baker opened opposite it a commodious double-fronted one for his hairdressing business, continuing there till forced by circumstances to move to High Street.

Jutting out far beyond Mr. Baker's and into Le Grand Carrefour (at the top of High Street) was Messrs. Dorey and Barringham's drapery and carpet emporium. A flight of several steps led up to the entrance which pointed in the direction of the Town Church.

---

2   I have since (September, 1933) learnt through a friend that these two ladies were sisters, Mrs. Thomas and Miss Riskey.

Smith Street, looking down towards High Street

15

High Street and Town Church

The first building on its right in High Street was Mr. Greenslade's grocer's shop which, too, had a few steps in the doorway, the bottom one, perhaps, encroaching on the footpath. The windows of the shop, like those of many others in the town, were bowed and filled with ordinary panes of glass. Mr. Wm. Jones, sen., took Mr. Greenslade's place, his sons continuing the business until Mr. Pearsall bought it and some years later sold it to Le Riche. The archway across Lefebvre Street joined, on its other side, Mr. Worley's china shop, later carried on by Mr. Biggs, Mr. Noel, and Mr. Le Couteur successively. Next door to it came Madame I. Béghin's French glove, French boot, and fancy depot, which had been kept by her mother, Madame Gillet. It was replaced by Mr. Gale's boot shop and, afterwards, by Tyler's. Mr. Huxster, pastrycook, kept the shop beside it. Adjoining Mr. Huxster's were two others that projected half-way across the street and which were not thrown back for many years. Mr. Maguire, bootmaker, occupied the first of them, while Mr. Richard Arscott had the other for his piano warehouse. In the big house close to Mr. Arscott's, Mr. T. Turner carried on his drapery and costume business, one of the most important in the town. It became La Maison Cohu, Mr. and Mrs. Cohu (née Parry) having previously been members of the staff of Mr. Alfred Agnew. In Prince of Wales' House was Mr. W. Crousaz,[3] draper, Jurat Crousaz, his son, joining and succeeding him in business. Their name sounds strange to Guernsey ears and has excited wonder, but I believe that Jurat Crousaz' family came originally from Lausanne, in Switzerland, one hundred and fifty years ago. I may say in passing that both these gentlemen in turn were able organists at the Parish Church. Albert House was Mr. Cyder's clothing shop and near him was Mr. Giffard, ironmonger, whom Mr. John T. Lainé succeeded, followed by Mr. R. G. Agnew. At one time, Mr. Lamb, furrier, occupied that which is now Mr. Creighton's. On the other side of Berthelot Street, an old-fashioned establishment – that of Mr. Peter Roussel, wholesale grocer – preceded the States' Savings Bank. Mr. Roussel was an enlightened Jurat and took great interest in primary education. Mr. James Barbet's toyshop – now Dubras' hairdressing establishment – next to it must have existed for well nigh a century, his aunt, Miss Henry, having kept it before him.

---

3   Mr. Hamilton, a tall slight man, was a valued assistant there.

His daughter followed him and was succeeded by the Misses Grace whose father was a sea captain. Mr. Barbet was tall, but very far from stout. A public house for many years, and for long considered out of place in High Street, formed the corner leading to the Arcade. At the opposite corner, before Messrs. Bachmann and Co.'s premises were built, a shop with two bowed windows and its entrance in High Street and a bowed window in the Arcade as well, was occupied by Mr. Robin, cheesemonger, and father of Miss Gallienne Robin, authoress. It had, I think, a wider front than Mr. P. Roussel's, yet resembled it in general appearance. There was a pillar at each side of the doorway and at the other ends of the windows. Mr. Greenslade's, I think, had pillars like them. Mr. Thomas Grigg, carver and gilder, carried on his business a door or two below. Dick's shop was in High Street when I was quite a child and gutta-percha was first mentioned in connection with it. Mr. Mourant's drapery establishment is very old. Mr. Leak, sen., the oldest employee of the present owner's grandfather had been with him for fifty years, and that is long ago. The last shop on that side of the street was kept by Mr. Taudevin, a short and elderly man whom I never saw without spectacles and a soft felt hat. He dealt in toy boats and their fittings – we had few "model yachts" in those days – fishing tackle, small brass cannon and shell work. Quay Street, facing Mr. Taudevin's, was then in a very bad condition. Victoria Hotel, kept by a Mr. Brooks, I think, before Miss Green,

Abraham Bishop, Victoria House, High Street

stood opposite to Mr. Mourant's place of business. A large single-fronted shop adjoining the hotel was that of Mr. Angel, tobacconist, a tall and bony man, who had for next door neighbours Messrs. Dorey and Rougier, drapers, Mr. Rougier's son, a tall, dark, and very gentlemanly man[4] conducting an extensive tailoring business in a single-fronted shop beside his father's and where Mr. Torode had been before him, while Mr. Alfred Agnew (previously Jehan and Agnew), silk mercer and draper, with a considerable dressmaking department, had spacious premises on the present site of the London and Midland Bank.[5] Mr. Abm. Bishop's (Victoria House) drapery and costume business[6] was

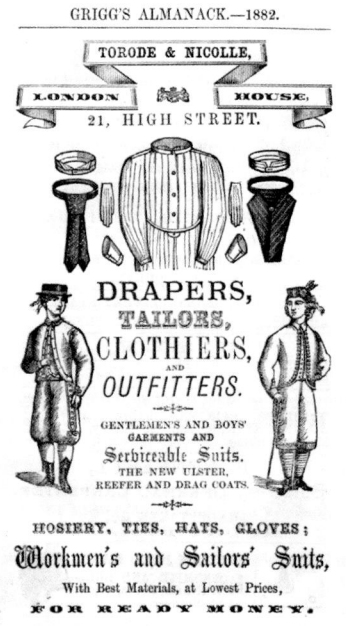

another old one and had existed before my time. Mr. Stephen Bishop, his eldest son, who went to Bristol, made several pretty model steamers as a hobby. In London House, adjoining Mr. Bishop's and facing Berthelot Street, Messrs. Torode and Nicolle, the one a dark man of ruddy complexion, the other taller and very fair, were in partnership as tailors and dealers in ready-made clothing. Messrs. de Carteret and Le Patourel[7] were assistants there for many years. Next to London House, in the shop now occupied by Mr. F. G. Fuzzey, dealer in pianos, gramophones, etc., was Mr. Bidmead, tobacconist. Mr. Bidmead was of low stature and always wore a dress hat in his shop. He was an active little man and his business a very good one.

Tobacco and cigars cost much less then. "Princesses" and "Queens",

---

4   Mr. Ogier, Mr. Robin and a Mr. Cohu were his shop assistants.

5   Mr. Verinder, the Misses Parry, Mr. Cohu and, later, Mrs. J.J. Reynolds (née Digard) were important members of his staff.

6   Has been sold to Messrs. Creasey & Son who (May-Aug, 1933) are making extensive alterations to the premises. Mr. Brehaut and Mr. Valpied were members of the staff for very many years. The former, though old, is (Aug. 1933) still living in good health.

7   Now (July 1933) themselves giving up business. Mr. de Carteret is in his 81st year (Feb. 1934). Mr. Le Patourel, not quite so old, has with Mrs. Le Patourel and their daughter gone for a cruise to South Africa.

two small cigars were sold at 1/8 and 1/3 per 25 respectively. The latter was the price of "Vevey fins". The best "Havanas" could be had, I think, for 3d. each. Tobacco was half what it is now. The States' Electric Showroom was Mr. Stephen Barbet's stationer's and bookseller's repository – Mr. James Barbet of the toyshop was his cousin, I believe – Messrs. Staddon and succeeded him and were followed, after several years, by Mr. F. B. Guerin,[8] son-in-law to Mr. Grigg. Waterloo House was the home of another long-established business. It was conducted in my time by two brothers, Messrs. Jno. and T. Carré, but I have heard my father say that it had before been under the style of Carré and Nephew, many people mistaking the latter for a surname. The Old Bank[9] – now the National and Provincial – has undergone extensive alterations. It had in front a shop, I think, which Mr. E. Le Lacheur and his son tenanted as watchmakers and jewellers, Mr. E. Béghin taking it for fancy goods after Mr. Le Lacheur, jun., had gone out of business. Over this shops were chambers occupied by Mr. J. B. Marquand,[10] écrivain. The one between the Old Bank and the Commercial was Mr. R. Cohen's tobacconist's, with another excellent business. Like its neighbour, the Commercial Bank[11] has been much altered and enlarged, and has for some years been a local branch of the Westminster. The shop next door above it which had been Mr. Edwin Winter Dupuy's, a chemist who married Mr. Stephen Barbet's daughter, was incorporated in the new building. Mr. J. Burwood's boot shop was the next one, Mr. E. N. Westever's a draper's shop above, and then one came to Mr. Millington's, a bookshop

---

8   Miss Grigg, his sister-in-law, and Miss Ferguson assisted him.

9   I knew Mr. Joseph Collings, Mr. Fred Hutchisson, Mr. Macey Jones, Mr. Chas Vancour, Mr. J.B. Collings(?) and Mr. E. Lainé there as managers.

10   Died at Norton Bavant, April 16th, 1934, aged 87.

11   Mr. Alfred Mansell, of "Ashgrove", Charroterie; Mr. Tardif, of Hauteville; and Mr. Alfred Marquand, of "Shorncliffe", Rohais, were successive managers.

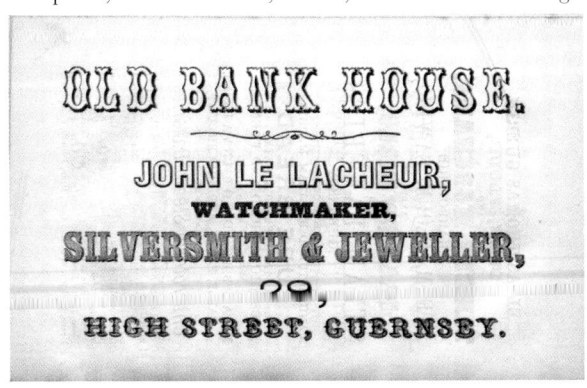

Le Grand Carrefour, junction of High Street and Smith Street

which became Stickland's and, later, Banks'. Another tradesman of the time was Mons. Chotin, a stout man of rather more than middle height. His was a perfumery and fancy business, I think, conducted on the same premises as his wife's millinery one, next door to Mr. Gray, whose shop adjoined the archway at Pier Steps. Mr. Gray was, in those days, the fashionable hairdresser and had a very good connection. A contrast to his neighbour, Mr. Bidmead, his height was quite remarkable, while he was very slim. On the other side of the archway, Mr. Baker continued his business when obliged to move from Smith Street to make room for the building of The Capital and Counties (now Lloyd's) Bank. Mr. Mauger, who married Mr. Bidmead's widow, had a draper's shop next, I think, to Mr. Baker. Mr. E. Bachmann, watchmaker and jeweller, who had started business in the lower part of Vauvert Road, moved to a shop in High Street by Mr. Baker's before going to his present premises and may have preceded Mr. Mauger, but the alterations made since then have blotted the exact spot from my memory. Mr. H. Crousaz, brother to Mr. Crousaz of Prince of Wales' House, carried on a wine and spirit business at the Yacht Hotel[12] which Boots recently acquired for their chemist's and fancy business. Mr. Powell succeeded him and eventually disposed of the goodwill to Le Riche.

---

12   I believe that it was in this house that Sir Isaac Brock was born.

The Pollet

The Pollet has some interesting memories and though much altered still retains some traces of the past. Mr. H. Cumber's pharmacy, at No.3, must have witnessed many changes for, in my earliest years, this gentleman assisted by his widowed sister, Mrs. Sharshaw, mother of Mrs. James Gardner of the Royal Hotel, conducted it on the same premises as his descendants now. Mr. Cumber, jun., his grandson, was kind enough to show me recently a framed document attesting that his great-grandfather and Mr. Le Quesne, his partner, were practising as chemists in 1826, Mr. Cumber informing me that they were at the time in Cornet Street.

Mr. T. A. Grut, photographer, who had been operator for Madame Javelot in the lower part of Victoria Road and was afterwards with Mons. André of No.2, Victoria Crescent, higher up on the other side of the same thoroughfare, and whom he succeeded when the latter left the island, opened, later, the studio which Mr. Norman Grut, his son, still carries on, but in which he has made alterations. Messrs. Hitchins and Son, wine merchants, were next door to Mr. Grut, while Mr. Foster, tinsmith, plied his trade next door to them. Another tinsmith, close by, was Mr. Guest. Next to Mr. Foster was a grocer, Mr. James Street, who was at one time in Sir William Place, Truchot.

Opposite the Queen's Hotel, there were three residences,[13] in the uppermost of which lived the late Sir Edgar MacCulloch. The next was occupied by Mons. L. Constantin, father of Dr. O. Constantin, so widely known in later years as a medical practitioner. The Working Men's Association adjoined the last of these three houses. Their entertainment hall was up a broad flight of stairs – which started just inside the doorway – and extended over the two shops of Mr. J. Cressard (now Mrs. Machon's), cabinet maker and furniture dealer. In the last shop of the Lower Pollet – known formerly as La Tourgand – on the right when going down, Mr. A. P. Roger, jeweller, commenced his business while I was yet a youth and I remember that much earlier still, Mr. Waterman, a baker, was opposite. The site on which the Sarnia Fruit Co.'s premises have been erected was, in

---

13   Shop fronts have of late years been put in them.

Arthur Maunder, cycling champion

my boyhood, that of one of Messrs. James Keiller and Sons' factories[14] which had a yard beside it. Who carried on the Queen's Hotel, I cannot now remember. It has changed hands several times. Dr. B. Collenette practised at La Plaiderie and was succeeded by Dr. Dobie who sold the practice to Dr. Connellan, I think. Mr. Maunder's business in bicycles grew with myself and was established long ago. It is now the oldest in the Channel Islands. Mr. Maunder, with Mr. "Steve" Duquemin, Mr. A. Blake and others, was prominent in bicycle races, which, when I was twenty, formed the island's chief excitement.

The new machines with two wheels of a size created much astonishment and were by some regarded dubiously, so used were we to cycles with a high wheel and a very low one, several of which were still about, while Mons. P. D. François rode what was known as a "velocipede" – a machine with four. Mr. N. Ferguson's wine and spirit store has been incorporated with Messrs. Wyatt's (haberdashers) premises, though the projecting portion at the side with a low doorway and staircase is still preserved. It may be an interesting digression to recall here the conscientious manner in which Mr. Ferguson and Mr. T. Turner of High Street attended Parish Meetings. They were not content with slipshod methods, but duly weighed every proposition before voting.

Mr. Collins's premises have, with the widening of that end of the street, undergone great change in recent times. A French produce dealer, by name, Alphonse Mahaut, kept the shop when I was a boy. Mr. Collins took it after him, I think, and has been there more than fifty years. He is now nearly eighty.

---

14   The other and larger one was in Park Street (Rue du Pré), nearly opposite the Town Mills.

The Pollet

Market Square, with Commercial Arcade in the background

The Commercial Arcade & Market Street

The Commercial Arcade and Market Street may now claim our attention. Mrs. Burr, a dealer in art pottery, Bohemian glass, and furs, had a shop near the High Street opening of the Arcade, and on the right. I am inclined to think that it was in Maison Carré, but am not quite sure. The business, after many years, was moved to one of the two shops between Mr. Cox's and Taylor's Restaurant, her granddaughter, Miss Manning, marrying Mr. P. Hackett. Madame Aubert, milliner, was near Maison Carré also, for some years, but transferred her business afterwards to the shop on the further side of Mr. Abraham Brouard's. With "a sister", Mrs Le Huray, "to assist her", Maison Champion – their maiden name – was carried on for a long period. Mr. Paint (Paen), chemist, was another in the row and had Miss Vincent, bookseller, and sister to Mrs. Le Lièvre of the Star office, for neighbour at No.25. Mrs. Le Noury was then in Contrée Mansell. Mr. Rowe, sen., jeweller, and successor to Mr. Allen, his father-in-law, was next to Miss Vincent. Mr. Abraham Brouard's grocer's premises have become those of Messrs. Mackay and Co., wine and spirit merchants, and have been greatly altered. Mr. Brouard, with his two sons, used to do an extensive business with people from the country parishes, especially on Saturdays, when his shop was crowded. A venerable-looking man of middle height who also – in his latter years, at least – wore a dress hat in business, Mr. Brouard used patois largely with his customers and, in his day, was one of our chief tradesmen. Mr. Lihou's restaurant, which had been Mr. Hunkin's draper's shop was, in the old days, the chemist's shop of Mr. Allez, brother of Mr. Bredthaft Allez, écrivain. Both were tall, spare men. Mr. Lamb, furrier, occupied for many years the shop next to it, while Mrs. Jago, taxidermist, had the corner one which the late Mr. A. Le Cheminant adapted for his glass and china depot. Mr. Arnold, chemist, succeeded by Mr. A. Collenette who had for long assisted him, was two doors from the opening to the flight of steps to Clifton, his confrère, Mr. Edgar Dupuy being in business beside him.

Mr. Edgar Dupuy was Mr. Edwin Winter Dupuy's younger brother but did not much resemble him. It is true that both were dark, yet Mr.

Commercial Arcade

Edgar was a tall, slight man, whereas Mr. Edwin, of no more than middle height, was stout. The shop at the corner opposite was kept, long ago, by Mrs. Daddo and her daughters, one of whom was blind, as a ladies' drapery and baby linen warehouse. It is hardly recognizable in Mr. A. P. Roger's establishment. Mrs. Staddon, milliner, side by side, I think, with the Misses Ollivier, milliners, and Mr. Black, pastrycook, conducted their respective businesses, in shops which lay between Mrs. Daddo's and the corner facing Mr. Allez which, until recent years, was Mr. Paint's, the jeweller. This gentleman's proportions would attract notice, for he was far above the average man in size [15] Between Mr. Paint and the Central Passage came Mr. F. Le Cheminant, a grocer. Forming the opposite corner of the Passage, Mons. and Mme. Lacombe's shop held a good position for the sale of French slippers, toys, and other articles. A blank wall, used for posters, almost filled the gap between Mons. Lacombe's and the back of Mr. Robin's, cheesemonger's. "Arcadia" and shops have since been built there.

Down the Central Passage, and where Mr. Jackson, jeweller, is now, stood the first Post Office that I remember (about 1007). Business was

15   His brother, the chemist, was only half as big.

transacted through openings made in the partitions of a lobby some 8ft. or 10 ft. square. It was not till I was twelve or fourteen years of age that a new Post Office was opened at the end of the opposite side where now there is a restaurant,[16] the premises including those of the bookseller next door. The Postmaster in those days was Mr. Le Messurier, sen., who later lost his sight. Mr. Smith, gasfitter, and the first dealer in bicycles, who was followed by Mr. A. Blake in the same line of business, took, a few years later, the shop that faces one in the alley alongside. Mrs. Stribley (née Gaved), milliner, and Mr. T. H. Wheadon, hairdresser, before he took up growing, did business near Monsieur Lacombe. A shop which has changed hands several times in latter years and at present in the occupation of Mr. Bennett,[17] radio engineer, was in my childhood and for many years, that of Mr. Cox, bootmaker, whose eldest son succeeded him. He had, besides, a small shop opposite, which was demolished when the New Market was built, for there had been a lane running from the Arcade to the Town Church. At one time, Mr. David Marquand, tobacconist, noted for his fine bass voice, carried on business in a shop which faces the Market Steps and adjoined Mr. Cox's. I once heard his son sing at a Guille-Allès Concert and found his timbre to be more melodious than that of the professional engaged.

---

16   Has lately (June[?], 1933) become Henry's gâche shop.

17   He has (Aug. 1933) moved again to 13, Arcade.

Market Steps

The Market Steps have twice been widened, I believe. There was, if I remember rightly, but a single flight of rougher steps at the time I write of, and porters' trucks, it seems to me, were often left beside them.

In those days, the Rectory House was occupied by Mr. Myers, a retired actor who let apartments and who took photographic portraits. It was turned into a shop for Messrs. Osborne, tea merchants, forty years ago, a business that was, I think, the forerunner of Mr. Spong's – now Pontin's – in the Arcade. Mr. J. H. Parsons, fruiterer and seedsman, was on the same site as his present kinsman, but in more modest premises which underwent extensive alterations a little later than the Rectory House. Next to Mr. Parsons was Mr. Hodder, hatter. "Shiny hats", as they were called familiarly were, then, often met with, especially among schoolchildren. A low flat hat like a straw one, but made of waterproof material. A passer-by chancing to wear a hat of this description might hear an urchin shout:

If you want to buy a hat, don't you buy a 'shiner'.
Go up to Mr. Gibson's shop and get a four-and-niner.

The main entrance to the Guille-Allès Library was not yet built. A broad paved space permitting free passage to and from the French Halles, with a raised shop at the back of it, existed on the site. This shop was occupied by Mr. G. Brand, fishmonger, poulterer, and game dealer, who did an extensive

Building the entrance to Guille-Allès Library

French Halles, Guernsey.   Guerin, Publisher.

French Halles or Leadenhall Market

business. Mr. and Mrs. Ferguson succeeded him, moving later to what is now known as "The Fisheries" in the States Arcade. There was a corresponding space where the Poids de la Reine at present stand, with a public house, bearing the name of "Golden Lion", on higher level.

The French Halles, called also the Leadenhall Market(!), were devoted chiefly to the sale of eggs, vegetables and poultry which came from France. A few women wearing their Norman or Breton head-dress might still be seen there when I was very young. Because of her remarkably tall cap and from the fact that she had one of the shops along the back wall of the market, so that you could not help seeing her, Mme. Rose Collivet was the most noticeable among them. The others had tables. She was, I think, the last of these stall-holders, for she was still in the Halles long after I had grown to manhood. Others holding stalls were Mrs. Abraham, Mrs. de la Cour, Mrs. Oliver Le Duc, mother of Mrs. W. J. Austin, the ex-Court usher's wife, and Mme. Dumont, a little woman with a very tall cap. Although, as I have said, this Market was allotted to those who sold French produce, Mr. Samuel Best, butcher, had two shops there for many years – at the end next Mr. Brand – and very much disliked the change to the New Meat Market. Mrs. Sebire, a Guernseywoman, sold fruit and vegetables in one next him. Mrs. Irish who had long carried on a basket business in a passage by the Rectory House and now occupied by Mr. Wardley's staircase, took afterwards the shop, I think next Mrs. Sebire, while Mr. I. C. Fuzzey's mother was stationed at the

31

corner where there is an entrance to the Guille-Allès Library. Mr. Tucker was proprietor of the Market Hotel, also known as Coles', which became the Artizans' Institute some years after Messrs. Guille and Allès had established their Library in the old Assembly Rooms where balls, bazaars, and other functions had previously been held.

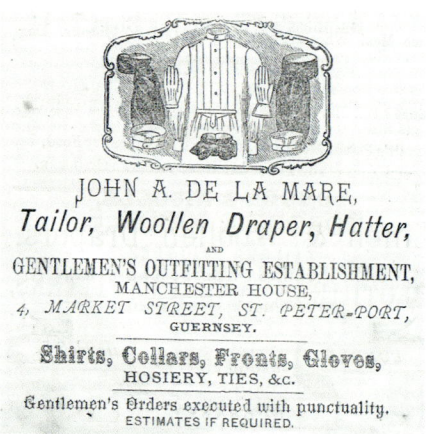

JOHN A. DE LA MARE,
Tailor, Woollen Draper, Hatter,
AND
GENTLEMEN'S OUTFITTING ESTABLISHMENT,
MANCHESTER HOUSE,
4, MARKET STREET, ST. PETER-PORT,
GUERNSEY.

Shirts, Collars, Fronts, Gloves,
HOSIERY, TIES, &c.

Gentlemen's Orders executed with punctuality.
ESTIMATES IF REQUIRED.

Mr. John Le Cheminant, grocer, and brother of Mr. Le Cheminant of the Central Passage, carried on business in the shop beside Clifton Steps. My father used to tell me that he had known a Mrs. Baxter there who dealt, I think, in carpets among other things. Mr. Le Cheminant was succeeded by his daughter, Mrs. Martel, and her husband. He had for next door neighbour Mr. Robin who was a grocer also. Then came Mr. de la Mare, hatter, hosier and tailor. Until he moved to Le Bordage, when Mr. R. D. Leak, a grocer, took the shop, Mr. Jas. Carré, sen., chemist, a brother of the gentleman of Waterloo House, High Street, was between Mr. de la Mare and Constitution Steps. Mr. Ray, sen., watchmaker, and, later, Mr. Levi Spiller of the same trade, followed his occupation in the small shop on the other side of the Steps. Mrs. Weeks, tobacconist, was next to him, while Mr. Gruchy, whose nephew, Mr. Chas. Gruchy de la Mare, was in later years a familiar figure at the Guille-Allès Library, carried on business as a leather cutter and dealer in grindery in the place now held by the "Golden Lion". The big house known as "Murdoch's Stores" was, then, occupied by Mr. Mansell Mauger and his family.

On the other side of Market Street there stood, before the New Fish Market was built, a row of smaller houses with a passage into Fountain Street between it and the end of the Meat Market. Mr. Pengelley, grocer, etc., used one or two of them until the building of the Fish Market when, transferring his business across the street, he preceded Mr. Murdoch in those premises. His carts, and those of Bucktrout, were of the kind then used by certain bakers – Mr. Swaffield of Victoria Road, for instance – a large square-covered box with rail around the top except in front, where the driver was seated. Rotund in form and rather short, Mr. Pengelley himself was somewhat remarkable, standing on the doorsteps of the "Stores", as was his wont, with one hand in his trouser pocket.

At that time, the seats which, until recent years, were fixed in the arched recesses outside of the Meat Market were used by Guernseywomen selling butter.

In the States' Arcade were to be found Mr. Naftel, chemist and brother of Paul Naftel, a well-known local artist; Mr. Frederick Clarke, sen., grandfather of the present occupier of the premises; Mr. Mould, sen., saddler, who had, I think, succeeded Mr. Vincent of the trade. In later years, Mr. C. Mellish, chemist and younger brother of Mr. T. Mellish who was in the Constables' Office, succeeded Mr. Naftel and gave way in time to Mr. de la Rue.

At the west end of the balcony above and at a right angle to it, a long room was the Mechanics' Institute, a kind of predecessor of the Guille-Allès Library. Mr. Ahier, a former candlemaker, and at one time a wealthy man, filled the position of librarian. The late Sir Edgar MacCulloch; Mr. J. B. Torode, écrivain; Mr. H. Crousaz; my father; Mr. J. B. Randell; Mr. Derrick, and a host of others frequented it. A corresponding apartment at the other end of the balcony was used as the Museum,[18] but I do not remember who had charge of it. Those exhibits which were still in good or fair condition were afterwards removed to more suitable accommodation in the Guille-Allès building.

Before the New Market was erected, the Market Square was the emporium for vegetables. The farmers' wives in numbers sat there surrounded by all sorts of baskets and denerel measures – made by local coopers – with quart and pint metal mugs as well, a big umbrella sheltering them from showers or a too ardent sunshine. A sweetmeat stall stood here and there among them. One belonged, I think, to Mrs. Nicolle of Le Petit Carrefour. Mrs. Green, of Back Street, placed hers before the Rectory House. A third was Messrs. J. Keiller and Sons' property, I think, while Mr. Sheriff had a fourth. On all sides, Guernsey-French was to be heard as well as English. On Saturdays, Mr. Martin, whose nursery was near the Câtel Church, arranged the fruit trees that he had for sale against the railings of our parochial place of worship. Two francs, I think, was what he charged for pear and apple trees, for my father used to patronize him.

To the South and East of the Town Church, there was then a block of three large houses, of which the biggest – facing East – had a projecting portion in front supported on stout pillars with railings between them that encircled a small sunken yard before the entrance door. It was here that Mr. Wm. Cadic, founder of Bucktrout and Co., did business before building the newer premises in Cornet Street. His next door neighbour was Mr.

18   This apartment was destroyed for the erection of the New Market.

Houses in front of the Town Church before their demolition in 1913

Stroobant, publican. The shop around the corner with its window looking towards Fountain Street was long the Maritime Inn kept by people of the name of Mauger, and, at a later period, became Mr. Jory's charcuterie. The Rev. G.E. Lee when he was Rector strove for many years, I think, ere he succeeded in getting this block of buildings demolished, to the great advantage of the beauty of the church.

The Picquet House was our first Telegraph Office, telegraphic communication with England and, I think, with Jersey also, being set up in 1870.

In Church Square, Mr. A. C. Quick, bootmaker, occupied the shop pointing towards the North door of the church. His son joined him afterwards. He was taller than his father and was slight instead of stout. Mr. Haize, a saddler, opened business, too, in a new shop on the East side of the Square.

Bucktrout's, Cornet Street, from Town Church

Fountain Street and entrance to Fish Market

FOUNTAIN STREET & LE BORDAGE

Crossing over to Fountain Street, Mr. de Jersey's ironmongery establishment would have been found first on the right. An archway to the Fish Market intervened between Mr. de Jersey's shops (now de la Rue's) and that of Mr. F. J. Weysom, grocer. One or two doors further on, there was a public-house.

The Fish Market itself was, in my youth, redundant with supplies from local sources. A good turbot might be bought for six francs, a brill for five francs, a pair of soles for two francs. Whiting and plaice were plentiful. Cod, mullet, and John dorys could be obtained, while spider crabs, chancre crabs, crayfish and lobsters were always to be found. Huge congers and conger eels were scarcely ever absent. Mackerel, in summer, flooded the Market. In short, our Markets in general were the admiration of all visitors.

Conger! I remember, by the way, was then the epithet applied to the young gentlemen attending the local Public School.

The Gazette and Advertiser office has not changed position since my childhood, but was considerably improved when I was a young man. A dyer, Mr. Webber, was formerly next door to it, in Fountain Street, Mr. Robin (now Anderson's), baker and confectioner, as well as builder, did business on the present premises, while, on the East side of the steps to Rosemary Lane, Mr. Mahy, popularly styled the "French" baker – from the form, I think, of many of his loaves, or because he took over De Bertrand's, a French baker's business – had a large connection in his line. Mr. T. W. Cluett, another baker, kept the shop at No.10, having there a boot and shoe establishment as well. Mr. Clothier and Mr. Goesle both had grocers' shops on this side of the street. There were, besides, three or four eating-houses, much frequented on market days. One of them was kept by Mme. Heuzé and another by Mr. Stedman, a brother of the cutter at Mr. Rougier's tailor's shop in High Street. A third was Coles', I think.

The chemist's business in Fountain Street, now carried on by one of Mr. H. Cumber's family was in my boyhood that of Mr. Satterley. Mr. Brouard and his sister continued it until it was taken over by Mr. H. Cumber's eldest son.

The States' Savings Bank at that time was situated in the premises where Barclay's is now established and for which they underwent some alteration. Mr. Amice Le Cocq, a very stout man of middle height was Actuary, Mr. F. Robin, taller but only a little less stout, Sub-Manager, and Mr. de Garis, a broad dark man with a long beard was clerk. The States' Offices were on the upper floors and were entered by the rear, under the archway in Cornet Street.

In Cornet Street, we may notice on the left, next to the old Sisters' Cemetery, the warehouse and cigarette factory of Messrs. Bucktrout and Co., successors to Wm. Cadic and, next door above, the Clarence Hotel, at one time kept by Mrs. Biddlecombe, Mr. James Gardner's sister. Lombardy House, a pawnshop, higher up, belonged to Mr. Symthson who had also been an actor. Until I was grown up, Messrs. Bucktrout and Co. carried on their business as grocers and wine and spirit merchants in Cornet Street. Mr. Hamel, sen., a tall spare man who had been with Mr. Cadic, Mr. G. Wheadon, with curly hair and who lived, I think, to eighty, with Mr. M. Hickey, were familiar figures in the shop. Mr. Bucktrout himself, a tall, slight man who did not live to a great age, had for sleeping partner, Mr. Whitehead, an architect, who was the designer of Brock Road Chapel. He, too, was tall but much more stoutly built than Mr. Bucktrout.

Cornet Street has been translated "Horn" Street and, until recent years, was commonly known as such, but I am under the impression that Cornet was the name of a family of note in former times.

The extensive new premises of Messrs. de la Mare and Co. in Bordage Street displaced several shops. Adjoining Nicolle's in Le Petit Carrefour were two tall houses with shops. Next to them was Mr. Grut, draper, and father of Mr. T. A. Grut, photographer. Mr. Grut was very fond of boating and might often be seen starting for a sail when business for the day was over. A tiny shop, Mr. Trouteaud's, watchmaker, with rooms above and steps up to the entrance, was wedged between Mr. Grut's and Mr. J. Cluett, baker.

With the widening of the street, the premises of Mr. T. H. Agnew have undergone great change, but his business was conducted there from my earliest recollection. He was a man of pleasant manner. In figure tall and rather slight, he was of dark complexion. He married Miss Le Page and had a large family, a few members of which are living. His eldest son went to Canada while a young man and became a prominent citizen of the town in which he settled. He has revisited the island on more than one occasion.

Le Bordage

Maison Blicq, beside Mr. Agnew's, dates back, perhaps, still further – 1848 – and, until the alterations, advanced into the street. Facing the inner end of the narrow passage between it and Mons. Dubras, hairdresser, a large French-looking house, "La Brasserie", may still be seen. The window shutters – in the lower rooms, at least – are of mahogany. Formerly, there was at the footpath a wide gateway to the yard in front of it. It was in this house that Sir Peter Stafford Carey was born. Upon the yard, two shops (!) were built when I was sixteen years of age, Mr. Gliddon, leather merchant, occupying the nearer one to Maison Blicq and Mr. Stafford, tobacconist as well as postman, the other. Mr. Ernest Robert, much later, took it for the same business, his elder half-brother, Mr. Robert, carrying on their father's as baker and grocer in a larger shop above. These were, however, all pulled down to make room for Tudor House and its annexes. The British Bakery and neighbouring shops replace some stores that once existed there. The last one, next to the pump, and, maybe, the last but one as well, was occupied by Mr. Amy, general merchant, and agent for Devenish and Co. I may say that Mrs. Amy kept a school, which had a reputation.

A Mr. Amies, wearing a long white beard, used, when I was very young, to come daily to the bathing-place. He introduced guano to the island.

39

Although I remember its odour, I was not old enough to trouble if it was keenly taken up or not. He was an older man than Mr. Amy, but both were corpulent and rather short.

The old salt stores beyond the pump belonged to Mr. N. Martel. Near them, Mr. T. Harris, with his sister, kept a wine and spirit store. A Cornishman, he was another sailor who had never learnt to swim until he left the sea. At the corner of the lane to Mansell Street, Mr. Victor Lequilbecq,[19] when I was six or seven, followed his trade of saddler. He had in his employ a Mr. Caines, or Kaines, I think, who very long survived him and carried on the business for some years, as Mr. Lequilbecq died prematurely owing, I have heard it said, to a cold contracted while assisting to put out a fire that had occurred in the Arcade. A signboard of his remained on the back wall of the premises until quite recent years. Mr. W. D. Murdoch occupied this shop when first he set up in business. The Charroterie Mills throughout my life have had a depot at the other corner. Mr. R. Masters held auctions periodically, until I was grown up, in the large yard adjoining. It became known as "Masters's Yard" though belonging to the proprietor of the Charroterie Mills, Mr. E. T. de Guérin. Mr. W. Luff's furniture business has remained in the same place as now for more than half a century. The stoneyard near was carried on, until some years ago, by Mr. B. Webber. Mr. Jas. Carré, sen., chemist, a slight man with Dundreary whiskers, had a large store opposite Mr. Lequilbecq's shop altered to make the present place of business. He was among the earliest, if not the first, in the island to make mineral waters, which he manufactured on the floor above, and for which he had a great demand. Mr. E. Paul, saddler, when later he set up in business was next door below, while his father, in the shop beside him, plied the trade of tin and coppersmith. The bakery beyond the "Harp and Crown" was in my boyhood kept by Mr. J. H. Ingrouille. It passed afterwards to Mr. Head and then to Mr. Cannon, from whom the British Bakery Co. purchased the business. Mr. Ollivier's gunsmith's shop, has, from my boyhood, been on Tower Hill, his father and his grandfather(?) having preceded him. Mr. Blicq, sen., hairdresser, set up at the top of Tower Hill and foot of Hauteville in 1847. Mr. Fox selling secondhand goods opposite. At the corner facing Mr. Ollivier, Mons. Jean Marie, whose wife was Mme. Guernier's daughter, sold French footwear and other goods. Next to him was Mr. Marquand, carver, and a man of talent in his calling. Near by was Mme. Martin's charcuterie, while Mr. Warr, saddler, carried on his business at the bottom of Tower Hill Steps, in a shop that has been much altered to form a branch of Le Riche's Stores. Mr. Whicker, toy and fancy

Mrs Nicolle's shop in the 'skyscrapers' at Le Petit Carrefour

dealer, and the Star Office were neighbours lower down, the small frontage of the latter being opposite the higher window and the side entrance of Leale Ltd. Miss C. White, a little woman, was usually to be found there.

Mrs. Nicolle's pastrycook's and sweet shop in the Petit Carrefour was established in 1845. The house, for Guernsey, is a "skyscraper", consisting as it does of no less than six floors. The business has always been a famous one and the old lady in her day, well known. I have often seen her. Dressed in Guernsey fashion, with a black cap or bonnet on her head, buxom Mrs. Nicolle was ready to serve all and sundry, her cheerfulness adding to the sweetness of her wares. Mr. Nicolle – of Torode and Nicolle, High Street – was her son. Mr. H. Moon, bootmaker, was another of Guernsey's old business-men. His house at the foot of Mill Street, now occupied by Mr. Cowley, tobacconist, vies in height with Mrs. Nicolle's. This fact reminds me that a Dr. Sheppard used every morning, as he returned from bathing, to ascend the steps beside it (!) – no doubt, to reach his home.

41

H. TURNER,

Bookbinder & Commission Agent,

7, Mill Street, Guernsey.

LATHES, FRET SAWS, BICYCLES, SEWING
MACHINES of the most improved designs. Circulars on
application. Sewing Machines Repaired.

Old Newspapers bought in small and large quantities.
Good price given for the "TIMES" and clean newspapers.

H. Turner, Mill Street (Le Lievre's 1884 Almanack)

Maison Le Noury, Contrée Mansell

42

MILL STREET &
MANSELL STREET

Mr. Thos. Robin opened, as a grocer's shop, the premises now used by Messrs. de la Mare and Co. for boots. Much earlier than that, Mr. Wm. Jamouneau, an excellent bookbinder, was to be found next door above. On coming to the island, more than sixty years ago, Mons. and Mme. Gilles Feuillerat began a French drapery business in the shop at present occupied by Mr. Le Lacheur as a grindery store. Mr. H. Turner, from Smith Street, came there afterwards, assuming, in course of time, the rôle of private detective while continuing his bookbinding. Though known as a good bookbinder, he rose to fame as a detective through his successful recovery of a travelling trunk lost on the journey by a passenger to the islands. For a long time, all efforts to trace the "missing links", and other things, had failed. At last, the owner, or a friend, appealed to Mr. Turner. Nothing daunted, this gentleman went off to England, returning with the box in less than three weeks' time, I think. About half-way up the hill, Mrs. Petherick, whose daughter and her husband, Mr. Renier, a little man, succeeded her, sold secondhand furniture in a large double-fronted house. It has since been divided into smaller shops, one occupied by Mr. Fisher, florist, and the other by Mr. Davies, chemist. Bordering Burnt Lane Steps, Messrs. Way and Sons had their paperhanging and decorating establishment. The eldest of the three sons was possessed of a good voice and used to sing in public under the name of "Fred Harcourt", I think. Mr. Ray, an aged watchmaker and jeweller, spoken of elsewhere, had at one time a shop in Mansell Street near Burnt Lane Steps. From my earliest years, Miss Masters, milliner and draper, conducted her business in the same premises as her successors do now. For some years her sister, Mr. Whicker's widow, assisted her. A little further on, Mr. W. Courtenay, watchmaker, and, later, manager of the Hon. Molesworth's farm, and Mr. C. Loaring, bootmaker, pursued their trades in small shops separated by a wooden partition. One of Mr. Wallis' two shops was close to them and next came Mr. Lihou, grocer and toy dealer, who towards the end of October in each year carried a good stock of squibs and other fireworks. Mr. Wallis' second shop separated Mr. Lihou's from Mr. Symes, furniture broker, who occupied two more. Many fine specimens of cabinet work passed through the latter's hands, while his shops were the resort of visiting, as well as local connoisseurs. Continuing a long-established plumbing business next door to Mr. Symes, in which Mr. Fleure had been his partner, was Mr. Webber, rather a big man. His son, a smaller one, joined him in time and succeeded him, retiring after many years and selling his connection. The next shop, apparently a fairly old one, for the date above the door is 1746, and now one of Messrs. Luff and Co.'s for whom the floor above it was removed, is that to which Mons. and Mme. G. Feuillerat, after a time, transferred their business from Mill Street. Mons. Feuillerat, a short, stout man with long black beard was also a tobacconist. Excellent olive oil might be obtained as well from their abundant stock.

Guerin's Almanack, 1899

Mr. Payne, gasfitter, occupies in Contrée Mansell Mr. and Mrs. Le Noury's old bakery and confectioner's shop. From Mrs. Clouting's to Vauvert Road everything has changed and, fifty years ago, the shops now there were not yet made. Mr. Day, a baker, did business in a house which Mr. Laventure's (now Hill's) shop replaced and Mr. W. Marquand, tobacconist and a brother of the carver, next door, in a house which formed the corner and was pulled down to afford room for the growing traffic up and down Victoria Road. The doorways of these houses were below the level of the street and had a narrow space in front of them enclosed by wooden railings. The building now used as a fish restaurant was erected on the site and, first of all, was occupied by a French chemist. A linen draper, whose name I am not sure of, took it afterwards for several years. The shop now kept by Mr. Adam, wireless dealer, was for long the seat of a fancy business conducted by Miss Langlois and Miss Luce.

In Mansell Court, the fine old house which Mr. Bennett – now opposite the Market Steps[20] – has just vacated and for whom the shop-front was put in, was off and on a greengrocery as well as dwelling. In my boyhood and my youth, the premises which Messrs. Stroobant and Symes, a little time ago, adapted for their hairdressing business were those of Mr. Gardner, a chemist,

20   Later (Aug. 1933) at No. 13, Arcade.

Mansell Court

who kept two Pomeranian dogs. Some people, in former days, bought tea at the chemist's and I have heard it said that Mr. Gardner had many patrons for this article. Later on, this place became "The Handy Shop" controlled by Mr. Hawke who had previously occupied one of the small new shops in Contrée Mansell. Around the corner, Mr. Shayer and, afterwards, his son, carried on the trade of tip-smith in the old low shop facing the North side of Holy Trinity Church. Mr. Shayer, jun., who strongly resembled his father in features and in tall figure, had been employed in Keiller's factories away making tin biscuit boxes. I hear that he died a few years ago in England, well over ninety years of age.

Returning along Mansell Street, an old-fashioned and double-fronted shop[21] stood opposite that of Mme. Feuillerat. Succeeding well, she took this shop, leaving the other to her husband for his tobacco business. The high-fronted one facing Mr. Lihou's toyshop was a second depot of the Charroterie Steam Mills, a tall man, Mr. Draper, or Dreaper, sen., having charge of it. Mr. Bush's baker's shop was, at that time, Mr. Bartlett's and, forming a corner removed about forty years ago, there was next to it a tiny shop kept by Mrs. Massart, umbrella maker. The floor above was reached by a ladder through a trap door in the ceiling. Miss Le Cheminant,

---

21   Great alterations were, much later, made in it to become "Marmain's Stores", which have since been taken over by Messrs. Luff & Co.

Marmain's Stores, Mansell Street

who became Mrs. George Baker, and who is still hale and hearty though advanced in years,[22] carried on a milliner's business in Mr. Haysom the jeweller's present shop for very many years.

When I was a boy and for a time afterwards, Mr. I.C. Fuzzey and Mr. Wm. Luff were in partnership as cabinet makers and furniture dealers in the store[23] beside the steps which has done duty ever since and is now connected to Tudor House in the Bordage. A Mr. Forward had, I believe, preceded them. From the small house next it to Mrs. Ozanne's (now Ozanne and Haysom) there was a wall about five feet high with a bakery beneath it. Messrs. Fuzzey's double shopfront replaced the wall a good many years since. On the premises of Hillman Ltd., Miss S. M. Phillips conducted a grocer's business Mr. W. D. Murdoch was her assistant before he set up for himself. The place has been much altered but, if memory be true to me, Miss Phillips' corresponded with Hillman's upper shop though raised above the street. In appearance greatly changed, the last shop but one is that in which the Messrs. Martin Bros. commenced business in tailoring and in tobacco. When they vacated it, Mr. Le Cheminant, a hairdresser, became the occupant.

---

22   Died April 5th, 1933, aged 94.

23   A storey is being erected over it (May 1933).

Keiller's Factory, Park Street

J.S. Sanders, Shoeing Smith, Trinity Square

Lovell & Cox advertisement, The Star, 14 July 1888

Trinity Square & Vauvert Road

More than fifty years ago, Messrs. Lovell and Cox (now Lovell and Co. Ltd.), cabinet makers and furniture dealers, opened business in Trinity Square, in the shop at present occupied by Mr. J. W. Renouf, grocer.[24] Mr. Petitt, also a grocer, had taken the place after them.

The institution of the Thursday half-holiday was largely, if not entirely, due to Mr. Lovell, sen.'s strenuous efforts which fructified some thirty years ago. It was long before he got his way, yet it appears to be a boon to the majority of those compelled to work indoors.

Somewhat earlier than Messrs. Lovell and Cox, Mr. Anderson had set up as a chemist at the corner of Upper Mansell Street where Mr. Thackrey is continuing the business. Messrs. Valpy and Son, iron-mongers, tenanted the premises which, later on, Mons. Y. Perrot, newsagent and tobacconist, took over and very much improved. On the other side of Vauvert Road, a carver and gilder's business was carried on by Mr. A. Grut who always seemed to walk with caution, as though suffering from corns. Mr. Le Carpentier, seedsman and forage dealer, had a shop and store beside the Bouillonne Steps and next to him Mr. Ozanne[25] succeeding his brother-in-law, Mr. Marquis, in the wine and grocery trade. Mr. Ozanne's shop was afterwards thrown back to render traffic safer and Mr. Le Carpentier's so altered that one could scarcely have believed that it had existed in the place of the modern shop of Mons. Genêt, baker.

At the other corner of Victoria Road, but with its front in Vauvert, a shop was occupied by Mr. Ralls, sen., cabinet maker, upholsterer, etc. The large shop and warehouse, in Victoria Road, adjoining it were erected in my youth. Mr. Ralls, a tall, broad man, with long white beard, and leaning on a stick looked venerable. Miss Henry's confectionery business had already existed some years, I think, for it had been opened by her aunt, or aunts, whom, as a boy, I have seen in the shop. A short, plump woman with black eyes, Miss Henry was very neat in her appearance. Her goods were of best

24   Since deceased, yet the name continues there.

25   Died March 30th, 1933, aged 88.

Vauvert, with Aubert on right hand side

quality, her gâche was highly famed, her patrons, drawn from every class, were very numerous. Facing her shop was Mr. D. Aubert's (now the Vauvert Hardware Co.)[26] ironmongery. It had before been under the style of Aubert and Ozanne or Ozanne and Aubert, I am not sure which. Mr. D. Aubert, sen., was a little man, whereas his elder son was bigger than most people. Like Mr. T. Angel, tobacconist, of High Street, Mr. Jno. de Mouilpied and others, Mr. James Aubert had been a schoolfellow of my father. By a second marriage, Mr. Aubert, sen., had another son, Dan, who, sad to say, died early, leaving a widow and two boys. His mother was Mme. Aubert, milliner, mentioned in my description of the Commercial Arcade. Mr. Le Cheminant, brother of Miss Le Cheminant of Mansell Street, was long a chief employé of the Vauvert firm. In the shop next to Salem Chapel and in the yard adjoining Mr. Aubert's premises, Mr. Taylor, dyer, had his business. It was a very good one, but declined owing, I think, to the facility with which it became possible to get things dyed away. A Mr. Shayer, whitesmith, bell-hanger, etc., carried on the forge opposite and was succeeded by Mr. Newbury, an adept at his trade. The store next door above provided Mr. Renouf, turner, with a workshop. Mr. Shirvell and his son were cabinet makers at the corner of Burnt Lane, in the shop at present occupied by Mr. Brennan, house furnisher. Mr. Dumaresq and his family lived at La Porte Vase, since named "Violet Villa". His daughter, long after, married Rev. —. Crane. The Messrs. Senner's shop, since altered, used to be the bakery of Mr. Sheppard. A little higher up, in Vauvert, a very curious dwelling-house projected, until forty years ago, some distance across the road.

26   Acquired (Oct., 1933) by Leale Ltd.

Le Bordage and Pedvin Street, from Trinity Square

The ground floor, if I remember rightly, was raised about four feet. The masonry supporting it sloped outwards and the door, between two ancient windows, was approached by steps. It was occupied by Messrs. Targett and Hicks, chimney-sweeps, Mr. Hicks residing there long after his partner. Mr. Pengelley, where Mr. Hall is now, was a well-known carpenter and builder. He was a tall, spare man wearing the customary dress hat about his work. He[27] was the father-in-law of Mr. James Aubert.

In Allez Street was a stoneyard – at that time (1865-80) the leading one – carried on by Messrs. Randell and Son. Mr. Randell, sen., came from Swanage, I believe. He married Miss Le Pelley, by whom he had, I think, two daughters and two sons, himself outliving his partner, the elder one. A daughter married Mr. Hutton, a clever photographic artist who did business at 10, Grange Road, and, later, at the corner of Candie and Upland Road.

In St. George Street, we had Mr. Hansford, shoeing-smith and father of Mrs. G. Wheadon. Short, broad, and good-looking, with a long fair beard, he seemed always cheerful. In those days, shoeing-smiths were busy men and Mr. Hansford among the busiest. He might, with his son – a taller man – be heard at work from 6.30 in the morning, the clang of hammers ringing on the anvil. At the bottom of the street was Mr. T. Young's (now Mr. Le Tissier's) stoneyard. Aided by his brother, he turned out much good work. In fact, our Guernsey artizans were mostly clever in their calling. His name may be seen attached to many headstones.

---

27   He, a Guernseyman, was not related to his namesake of Market Street, who came probably from Cornwall.

St Julian's Avenue, opened 1873

Gardner's Royal Hotel, Glategny Esplanade

THE BORDERS OF
THE TOWN

In days gone by, before the Court House was enlarged, there was a building at each end of it. To the south was the Theatre Royal and All Saints' Church stood on the North of it. A grocer's shop was to be found where now we have a Police Station, while stores, terminated by a smaller shop occupied the site of the Plantation in St. James's Street. The entrance to this little shop[28] was at the corner. Three or four steps were in the doorway, as the floor was lower than the road. Le Marchant Street ran from New Street (Rue Marguerite) beside this shop and behind the stores to a short flight of steps at the side of All Saints' Church. Dr. Roberts lived at St. James's Place. Where Mr. Hamson is, Mons. Arséne Garnier, a short and very thick-set man and, until Mons. André came, our foremost photographer, carried on his business.

In Candie Road, a good-sized residence stood, until about forty-five years ago, on the small plot outside the lower entrance to Candie Grounds.

St. Julian's Avenue was, I think, commenced when I was about seven. I remember peering through the hoarding that stretched from Candie to La Rue aux Prêtres. Carriages to and from the harbour passed through Hirzel Street and the Truchot before the Avenue existed. I have heard that, cutting through much private property, it cost £10,000. There was, I think, a shipyard at the lower end, but I no longer remember clearly. A second, which was dismantled nearly fifty years ago, existed near La Salerie. Between the Battery and Salter Street there was a block of houses. It lingered some years longer than the shipyard but was eventually demolished.

The Royal Hotel,[29] in Mr. Gardner's time, was of moderate proportions, which may be discerned between the late additions. It is that part to which the name of the hotel is fixed and I remember a house, of which I have a photograph, that stood formerly on the site of the present dining-hall. Like that of Government House Hotel, its name has not been changed, whereas the "Channel Islands" was, years ago, the "Cambridge", kept by Mr. Cuell.

---

28   It was kept by Mrs. Bang, Sen.

29   Its tariff, later raised to 10/6, was in my youth but 7/6 a day!

Mr. Shirvell, jun., cabinet maker, opined that a hotel at 6/6 per day was needed for commercial travellers and opened the "Highlands" in Burnt Lane. His success there seems to have borne out his contention and to have encouraged him to take the "Cambridge".

In the outskirts of the town, there have been great changes since my youth. The ground now occupied by Dr. Collings' house and garden in Grange Road was, less than fifty years ago, a field belonging to Miss Carey who lived at Doyle Road corner opposite. During my early years, sheep were grazed in it and I recall that, as a child, I was greatly vexed at the impossibility of following their movements through the narrow chink between the gatepost and the gate, which was a solid one. There were then no dwellings beyond Lukis House. Miss Carey's garden wall alone filled up the gap between it and her own. In Doyle Road, this lady's property extended to Norfolk House (Ridout's Nursery), the greater part consisting of a field bounded by a wall quite eight feet high. The long, low house, Doyle House, was at the time the only one between the nursery and the corner of Doyle Road formed by a garden, the large house now standing there having been erected hardly forty years ago. Grove End and Connaught House were built about twenty years earlier, upon ground where Mr. Hambley, or Hambling, used to keep his stables.

Mrs Margaret Neve (1792-1903)

Rouge Huis Avenue, with all the houses from Road to Elm Grove, covers a large field that had a low wall[30] around it with a hedge and trees inside and which was not built upon till I was more than thirty. It belonged to Mrs. Neve, a lady who lived well over a hundred years[31] and was a near relative of General Harvey. Coronation Road was made, I think, soon after Rouge Huis Avenue. No thoroughfare from Amherst Road to Cambridge Park formerly existed. There was nothing but a wheelwright's yard where houses have been erected. It was Mr.

30 This has been retained in parts and openings have been made in it for gateways to the houses.

31 Almost to 111.

Rouge Huis House (Mrs. Neve's residence)

Gardner's, I think, for he had a wheelwright's shop facing Fosse Landry and lived at the left corner. The ground around Victoria Tower was very much neglected and years elapsed before a Plantation was made.

At that time, too, and for some years afterwards, a lane ran from Brock Road to Les Rocquettes, ending opposite General Mainguy's side gates. The Brock Road end may still be seen as part of Perchard's Stables. The upper part was bordered, on the left, by a high wall with a small doorway and formed the back of "Melrose". On the right, there was a ditch or stream, I think, a hedge extending the whole distance. Mr. MacGregor, the owner of "Melrose", obtained consent of the authorities to enclose this lane in order to unite his two properties, but on condition that he would build a wall – costing £800, I've heard – along La Gibauderie. It was said that he would have added "Rouge Huis" as well to his own place had Mrs. Neve been willing to part with it. Rosaire Avenue and Dalgairns Road have been made since then. Not very many years ago, a broad strip was taken from the garden of "Keppel Place" to widen Victoria Road. I have an idea that it was about the time of the arrival of the first motor buses. In the interests of motorists, the proprietors of "Les Gravées du Sud" and "Paradis" allowed the corners of their gardens, too, to be rounded off. The Grange Road was, autrefois, almost in a line with Les Gravées. The footpath in front of "Grange End", "Espérance" and "Edgeborough", much wider than the road itself, was, in my young days, a favourite meeting place on Sunday evenings after

Ivy Gates, Rohais, entrance to Les Granges de Beauvoir

service, and Guernsey's "capital", to some extent, "had gathered there her beauty and her chivalry". People chatting, stood about in groups, while others paced up and down. The roadway was considerably widened about thirty years ago, but leaving, still, a more than ordinary footpath, which was reduced, however, to its present limit within the last decade. In place of the public telephone and garden at the opening of Brock Road, there stood a detached house, called Varna House, about the size of "Ventnor", but with its gable towards the Grange and its front door facing East.

Valnord Bank, no more the same since I was ten or twelve, was then "Le Pelley's Field", full of mounds and hollows. Gladstone House, I think, was the latest to be built on it.

Other changes have taken place in a Westerly direction. Until 1890, or thereabout, York Avenue and Stanley Road were country thoroughfares. Isabelle Road dates back no further. A field, bounded by a wall breast high, stretched from "Verdala" to the corner. A second, much above the level of the road and bordered by a hedge with trees, extended from Ivy Gates to Foulon Vale.

At least another twenty years elapsed ere Richmond Avenue was made through Rev. Brehaut's property. This gentleman was, by the way, the first to build – quite sixty years ago – a bungalow at Cobo. Although of wood, it

Funeral procession of Lieut-Governor, Maj-Gen. Auld, 1911,
passing Varna House, The Grange

is still standing and seems to be in good condition.

Another part that is much changed since my boyhood and youth, Bailiff's Cross Road was, at that time, hardly built on, while corn was growing in the field which borders, also, the road to St. Andrew's.

Rev. Carey Brock (1825-1892)
Dean of Guernsey 1869-1892

Rev. Thomas Bell (1820-1917)
Dean of Guernsey 1892-1917

Rev. Nassau Cathcart (1828-1923)
Vicar of Holy Trinity Church 1861-1913

Very Rev. William Canon Foran (1845-1916)
Rector of St Joseph's Church 1873-1916

GENERAL TOPICS

Well-known people of my youth and early years were – Rev. R. J. Ozanne, Rector of the Parish Church; The Very Rev. Carey Brock, Rector of St. Peter-in-the-Wood and Dean; Rev. Thos. Brock, his brother, a most edifying man who was Incumbent of St. John's. He was tall in stature and wore a long beard. Rev. W. Collings, Seigneur of Sark; Rev. J. Oates, Principal of Elizabeth College; Rev. T. Bell, Rector of the Vale; Rev. J. Doyle Kennedy, Rector of St. Sampson's; Rev. J. Lakes and Rev. R. Walton Marmion, in turn Incumbents of St. James's Church; Rev. Nassau Cathcart, a tall man powerfully built who lived to a great age, Incumbent of Holy Trinity Church; Rev. Amadeus Guidez, the venerated Pastor of St. Joseph's, and, later, The Very Rev. William Canon Foran, besides other clergymen; Mr. Julius Carey, a very stout man of middle height and fond of music, at one time Chief Constable; Jurat Colonel de Vic Tupper, of "Les Côtils", Supervisor in succession to Jurat Tardif – Jurat Tupper, when a passenger on board the boat to Sark, would often take the steering wheel, for he held a pilot's licence, having passed the necessary examination in order the better to decide in cases brought before the Court – Colonel Wm. Bell, H.M.'s A.D.C. and Government Secretary, as big a man as his namesake of the Vale was small; Colonel de Vic Carey, of "Le Vallon"; the late Sir Godfrey Carey; J. de H. Utermarck, Esq.; Mr. W. Brock, of "Belmont"; Mr. Jno. Mansell, of Queen's Road; Captain Philip de Sausmarez, of Les Gravées; Mr. A. MacGregor, of "Melrose", usually driving a white horse in what was known as a "basket trap". Capt. de Sausmarez and Mrs. Lane Clarke,[32] of L'Hyvreuse, also used these convenient and comfortable carriages. Other familiar faces were those of Colonel and Mrs. McCrea, of "Grange Villa"; Miss de Lancey, of "Roseneath", Grange, a short, broad lady; Dr. Francis Carey who, when I was six or seven was, with Mrs. Carey, thrown out of his high gig in Les Ruettes Brayes and was rendered unconscious, I believe; Dr. M. A. B. Corbin and his daughters; Dr. Roberts, of St. James's Place; Dr. B. Collenette, of La Plaiderie; Mr. Joseph Collings; Mr. Alfred and Miss Ellen Collings; Mr. C. La Serre; Colonel Wellman; the Misses Farquharson, who lived, I think, in Hauteville; Rev. Perkins and his stepdaughters, the Misses Mordacque; as well as several others. Because of his swarthy complexion

---

32   Some people dubbed this lady "Queen Victoria" because she resembled Her Majesty
      in figure and, like Her, had blue eyes.

and of the handbag that he generally carried, Mr. Lauga was a gentleman who greatly attracted my notice. As a child, I met Victor Hugo in the street on one or two occasions. At this distance of time, my impression is that he was careless of his personal appearance and that his stature was but a poor criterion of his giant intellect.

Until 1883, when I became twenty-one, Sir Peter Stafford Carey, a rather tall slight man, was Bailiff. He had held office since 1845, a longer term than any of his predecessors, with one exception. His residence, much altered, particularly in point of architecture, has become the Candie Library. The wall enclosing it has also been replaced by iron railings.

The Sheriff was Mr. Stephen Martin, another tall thin man and, after him, was Mr. H. de Jersey Mauger who, while as tall as Mr. Martin, was somewhat stouter and had an extremely dark complexion which, with his long beard and the dress hat that he was in the habit of wearing, gave him an appearance suited to his office.

The Greffier whom I remember first was Mr. James Gallienne, a brother, I believe, of the late Rev. M. Gallienne, sen. He was immediately succeeded by Mr. Elisha M. Cohu, the Deputy Greffier, a smaller man than he but a most efficient Greffier, who was generally respected for his upright character. I may, perhaps, be permitted in passing to mention that he had a curious habit of sucking cloves, convinced that they would preserve him from colds.

I think that Mr. Utermarck was then the Procureur and the late Sir Godfrey Carey, Comptroller.

A familiar figure in the precincts of the Court was Mr. Wm. de Jersey. As Deputy Sergeant, he held office for a very lengthy period. So closely did he resemble Mr. Bidmead, tobacconist, in general appearance and in his predilection for a dress hat, that they might have passed for brothers.

So even was the tenour of our lives that it was not till I was twelve or fourteen years of age – and, perhaps, needed watching! – that we had more than two policemen, or "assistant constables", Mr. Williams, a man of middle height and broad – his daughter is the wife of Mr. Payne who is on the staff of the Charroterie Mills – and "bobby" Sarre, whose low stature and fussy ways excited the ridicule of the urchins of the town. Their uniform, retained for many years, consisted of a long frock coat and a dress hat with a line of tiny buttons down its side. These clothes seem rather hindrances than otherwise, but may, perhaps, have served to overawe possible offenders. The "force" was, later, doubled, Mr. Thoumine and Mr. Flambe being enrolled in addition to the others.

Sir Peter Stafford Carey (1803-1886)
Bailiff of Guernsey 1845-83

Victor Hugo (1802-1885)
resident in Guernsey 1855-1870

Dr. Benjamin Collenette (1814-1884)

Colonel William Bell (1830-1913)
Government Secretary 1868-1913

61

Promenade on the Jetty, St Peter Port Harbour, with Castle Cornet in the background

Concert in the Bandstand, Candie Grounds

AMUSEMENTS

Our pleasures were very simple, consisting chiefly of boating, bathing, and excursions to the bays[33] with, now and then, a trip to Sark or Herm. Sand-eeling on moonlight nights varied our amusements. Cricket was not organized, being but in the form of "bat and ball". Mr. Rowley's sons, I think it was, who, while at the College, gave the game great impetus. Football clubs were quite unknown when I was growing up. A skating rink was opened about 1877 at the bottom of Bosq Lane and, for some seasons, was well patronized, but bicycles, or other things, at last drew people from its floor.

It was a favourite practice of the townspeople to go to see the boat arrive from England which, in former days, was between half-past eight and nine. To those who had leisure, it gave an object to a morning walk, to those in business, an opportunity for healthy exercise ere the day's work began. It often happened that the boat came in, meanwhile, from Jersey, adding to the pleasure and prolonging the enjoyment. The Weymouth boat from Jersey in the evening – but only thrice a week, I think – was a further attraction to the harbour, which was much frequented when I was young. Roller skating, also, was permitted in the evenings for one or two seasons after the upper walk had been cemented.

The regimental band performance for two hours at Cambridge Park, on Tuesday afternoons, was another of our pleasures, but was, of course, by reason of the hour, restricted to the leisured classes. Attendance at this function was looked upon almost as a social duty. People met and talked, and walked about between the pieces of music. The bandstand was set up in the middle of the lower walk, the overhanging trees affording shade to players and to audience. A favourite band, among the rest, was that of the 22nd Regiment – with Mr. Bagnall, I think, for bandmaster.

Indoor Entertainments, in those days, began at 7.30, instructions to order carriages for 9.45 p.m. appearing on the programmes. Occasionally, a company from England would announce its bill of fare for 8 o'clock, but it was only after visitors had become more numerous and English ways had

---

33   To wash down the provisions we had taken with us, we used to buy there ginger beer
      in brown earthenware bottles and to pay 1d. for it.

begun to prevail that our local performances were retarded by half an hour. Clifton Hall – now occupied by the Salvation Army – used to be the place selected for entertainments appealing to the general public. St. Julian's Hall was not yet built and the Assembly Rooms (now the Guille-Allès Library) did not invariably find favour. The Philharmonic Concerts were held, perhaps, in either, but concerts in general, theatrical performances, certain bazaars, and conjuring entertainments usually took place at Clifton. The dwarfs, General Tom Thumb, his wife, Commodore Nutt, and Miss Minnie Warren appeared there when I was very young. At the South end of the Court House, until this was added to, we had a small theatre, the stage of which was pronounced by Mr. Wybert Rousby to be excellent, yet I presume that the building did not afford the necessary accommodation, for it was seldom used.

Commodore Nutt, Tom Thumb, Lavinia Warren & Minnie Warren

Lectures of various kinds, by Mr. A. Collenette and others, some concerts and, for a time, spelling bees, took place also in the Hall[34] of the Working Men's Association, Sergeant Butten of the Militia being a very popular comic singer.

Local playwrights appeared occasionally, while local histrionic talent betrayed itself at intervals. I call to mind a local comedy "The Belle of St. Saviour's" which was acted in several parishes and met with much success. A performance of "Box and Cox" at Clifton Hall, when I was eighteen years of age, attracted some attention, and was stated by the Press to be above the ordinary.

34   Channel Islands Exhibitions were held therein on two occasions. The first in 1868, and the other in 1872 (?).

After St. Julian's Hall was built, Clifton Hall declined in favour, though it continued for some time, however, to compete with the newer building. Livermore Bros.' Minstrels were, I think, among the first to adjourn to St. Julian's. The Two-Headed Nightingale occupied the boards for a couple of seasons and, later, came the operas of Gilbert and Sullivan.

Christmas Eve and the Queen's Birthday, as it was then, were the two principal events of the year. Among schoolchildren, the ditty ran:

> The 24th of May
> Is the Queen's Birthday.
> If we don't get a holiday,
> We'll all run away.

Bands might be heard from various quarters as the several regiments approached the Parade Field and people on the way enquiring of each other whether they had seen the "reds", or the "blues", as though they were talking of potatoes.

We had, when I was quite a boy, a rifle regiment in our Militia. It was less

St Julian's Hall (later the Gaumont Cinema)

"The Two-Headed Nightingale", conjoined twins Millie & Christine McCoy, c. 1867

Royal Guernsey Militia sergeant

strong than the other corps, but was looked upon as the smartest and the most select of all our local forces. Many of our chief tradesmen belonged to it. Mr. R. H. Randall, Mr. John Le Cheminant, Mr. Stephen Bishop, Mr. J. B. Randell, and Mr. Eugene Cadic were prominent among its officers. Mr. Stephen Bishop and Mr. J. B. Randell were enthusiastic marksmen and I think that the founding of the local "Wimbledon" was due to their exertions.

Militia service, in those days, continued to the age of forty-five, I think. Certain men were made "vingteniers" for a further period of five years, their duty being to warn for drill those on the active list.

Good Friday, strangely enough was, even then, considered as a holiday. From early in the morning – six o'clock or so – children could be heard shouting:

> One, a penny poker.
> Two, a penny tongs.
> Three, a penny shovel.
> Hot cross buns.

The first Monday in August, too, was the occasion of the Foresters' Demonstration. The mailboats coming from Jersey were packed with passengers and crowds assembled on the harbour to witness their arrival. Local members, with their band, went out to meet them and processions passed through the town to Cambridge Park, I think, or to a large field further out.

The 5th of November was availed of to let off fireworks and to burn the "boudelot" – a corruption, I believe, of "bout de l'an". Boys would go from door to door collecting coppers and the general excitement was much greater then than now.

The changing of the garrison was an "event" of former times. The

Boudelot Procession, St Andrews, 5 November, late 19th century

Himalaya and, I'm told, the *Crocodile* – no doubt, conveying tears for "The Girl I Left Behind Me" – used to come here as transports, very long ago. The last to come, on three occasions, was the *Assistance*, rendered necessary, of course, by the earlier struggles! She was a very ugly vessel. These transports were always anchored at some distance from the harbour.

Fire Engine at the Arsenal, 1935

Fire-fighting at the Quay, 1938.

Miscellaneous

Fires were, formerly, of very rare occurrence and, consequently, our fire engines, of which we had but two, I think, were not in first-class order. An engine, better kept, was stationed at Fort George and was brought to the assistance of our own when needed. The supply of water, too, was not always readily accessible. It was the custom for a row of men to line up on each side of the engine and to span the space between it and the nearest public pump, passing filled buckets up one line and, when emptied in the engine tank, to send them down the other. The earliest fire that I remember was that in the Arcade, to which I have referred elsewhere. I was then six or seven. Some years later, I believe, a squib thrown carelessly, set fire to a thatched house in La Gibauderie, opposite the present Dalgairns Road, while much later still, a house in Allez Street was burnt, Jubilee House replacing it. A few other conflagrations probably occurred, but I cannot now recall them. A friend tells me that there was one in Cornet Street and one in Rue A l'Or. Another person speaks of one in High Street about forty years ago when, he says, Mr. Arscott's music shop was burnt.

I assisted many years ago at a demonstration of the then new chemical fire extinguishers, given in the Candie Grounds before they were laid out as now. Long wooden trays packed with strips of wood were set in an almost upright position, a light being afterwards applied to them. When the mass was furiously blazing, a glass flask or two containing liquid was flung into it and quelled the fire immediately.

In this connection, I remember reading when I was young, a letter to *The Times* from Professor Albert J. Bernays in which he suggested that water from the hydrant might be pumped into a reservoir containing very soluble salts, such as Epsom-salt and others, and thence upon the fire. He contended that much less water would be necessary and that the even distribution of the chemicals would quench the fire more readily.

Are firelighters, by the way, like several other things, of Guernsey origin? I know that I was only eight or nine when Mr. Jory, in St. Julian's Avenue, was making them and that many years had passed before we heard of those of English manufacture. Mr. Jory's pattern consisted of a thick flat ring of pitchy substance with three supports of wood imbedded in it. If I remember rightly, he sold them at a halfpenny.

It used to amuse me, as a boy, to watch the lamp lighters – Mr. Trump and Mr. Bird were two of them – illuminate(!) our streets. Each carried on his shoulder a long light ladder, besides a lantern in one hand. On reaching a public lamp, he would run up the ladder rapidly, apply his lantern to the gas burner and, sitting astride his "mount", would slide down like a schoolboy to hurry off elsewhere. As time went on, the ladder was dispensed with and was replaced by a long staff, in the top of which the lamplighter inserted a match at every lamp he came to. Assembling under the archway at the opening of Lefebvre Street, the lamplighters started on

Commercial Arcade showing gas lamp

their rounds. It was Mr. Arnold who, while Manager for the Gas Company, introduced the automatic apparatus.

The Town Crier was another of our "public men" until I had grown up. "Jack" Trump, the scissors grinder, lamplighter, etc., a good-humoured "character", combined this office with his multifarious occupations. He was of an inventive turn and, at one time, had a boat which he propelled with paddlewheels connected with a crank inside the craft. I saw him also ride a "velocipede" of his own building, boys on the harbour teasing him by pushing him along.

Jack Trump, Town Crier

Excursion Car

Our dust carts, too, had formerly a bell in front of them. Livery Stables were numerous in those old days. Mr. G. H. Norton, in St. John Street, and, opposite him, Mr. J. Roberts – these places have become the Central Garage – Mr. Roberts, in College Street, Mr. H. Norton, in Ann's Place, Mr. F. Hooper, in Manor Place, and Mr. John Davey, at Les Croûtes, were all well-known proprietors. In Queen's Road, there was Mr. Bramwell. Mr. G. H. Norton, retiring, sold his business – the leading one – to Mr. Wm. Miller who, aided by his wife, daughter of Mme. Rose Collivet, greatly developed it, until he kept about one hundred horses – many of them in Brock Road.

Bath chairs were the most common carriages, but britskas and broughams were also to be seen, as well as many waggonettes of varying capacity. Excursion cars and landaus were not introduced until I was a youth, yet both were used some years earlier in Jersey. On Wednesdays and Saturdays, there were several waggonettes running to the country parishes to bring the people into town and to convey them home again. It was usual, I believe, for members of a family to take turns, so that each one might come in at least once a fortnight. Mr. John Davey supplied some of the largest of these waggonettes and got plenty of patronage. Crinolines were still in vogue and I remember how, when going for a picnic, ladies would brush these things aside to make room for a neighbour, as well as the vexation caused if a hoop should chance to break. Excursion cars, when introduced, went daily to the

In the Fish Market

harbour in order to book passengers arriving by the boats for tours around the island. "Nellie" Palmer, a big and well-built man, who was one of Mr. Miller's drivers, earned a reputation in conducting his car.

Patois was generally spoken among the Guernsey people till I was twenty years of age. The clattering of tongues on Saturdays was deafening in the Fish Market, so that I hated to pass through it.

Grotesque figures – some representing schoolmasters – formed with lobster shells, were common years ago. Mr. A. Le Cheminant and Mme. Lacombe in the Arcade had many of them. Mr. J. Barbet's toyshop and Mr. Taudevin's were places in High Street where others could be found. I had thought that they had entirely disappeared, but a young friend tells me that he has seen a few. There were, besides, dolls dressed as Guernsey market women, with a fichu and black cap or bonnet, surrounded by small hampers filled with tiny shells – many of them from Herm, most likely. These latter were exposed for sale in the shop of Mr. A. Grut, Vauvert, also. The making of both kinds of figures was a "home industry", I think. Visitors were struck by them and used to take them back to England.

The exportation of grapes is no new enterprise. It may have been conducted on a smaller scale, but Messrs. H. and W. Crousaz, Mr. Cox, sen., and Mr. H. Smithard sent away large quantities, the latter realizing at Christmas 15/- per lb. for his fruit. Years afterwards, Mr. Nightingale, sen.,

Grape Thinners

obtained, he told me, 7/6 at the same season.

Flocks of sheep were often met with when I was very young. A number were kept by Mr. S. Best at Les Ruettes Brayes, in the field dividing these from Colborne Road. Occasionally, a bullock cart would come to light, and I remember having seen, at times, a box-cart with a bullock in the shafts and a horse in front of him.

The "Clameur de Haro"[35] was not, as far as I remember, availed of until my early manhood, when Mr. H. Turner revived its use in connection with some alterations taking place in a house in Mill Street and which he feared would injure his business premises. The protest was effectual and matters were arranged to Mr. Turner's satisfaction. Twice since then, the clameur has been made use of to good purpose. First, to settle a dispute concerning railings opposite the façade of St. Paul's church and, lastly, in the widening of the Bordage, when the proprietor of Maison Blicq found his premises endangered during the demolition of an adjoining shop. In my youth, it seems to me, the "clameur" was referred to only as an old-time privilege.

Other recollections crowd in upon my memory! There were, formerly,

---

35   In the *Press* almanack for the year 1918, p.101, I came across the information that the
      fee assigned to the Bailiff for signing a "Clameur" is 5/-.

Ropewalk, St Johns, circa 1899

many artizans working on their own account. Cabinet makers, turners,[36] carpenters, coopers and carpet makers plied their trades in independence and made a comfortable living. Shoemakers who themselves made the boots and shoes were fairly numerous until I was more than twenty. Mr. Gale, in Vauvert, Mr. Maguire, in High Street, and Messrs. Lock and Son, St. John's, are names that I recall. "Blocks" for ships were still made in the island and we had several sailmakers. A ropewalk continued at Fosse Landry and another at Rouge Rue. Sawyers might be seen in action !

With a few exceptions, servants' wages at the time ranged from £8 to £16 per annum. The £ equalled 24 francs at the period. Charwomen earned 2 francs a day, I think, 4 francs was the usual pay of gardeners. People out of work could generally get stone cracking to do, earning 12/6 in the week, if I am not mistaken. The work was hard, of course, yet, at that time, this sum was not to be despised. There are several instances, I think, of parents having reared a family on stone cracking. Stone dressing was an exceedingly good trade, the pay reaching, I believe, £4 per week.

Sausmarez windmill, Ozanne's, in the Hubits, and another at La Hauteur, Vale, were still in use some thirty years ago, while it is not much longer since the waterwheels at Moulin Huet, Petit Bot, and Le Vrangue

---

36   Mr. Renouf, in Vauvert, also made mirrors, forcing mercury into sheets of plate glass
       with weights in the old way.

George Foote, veterinary surgeon

ceased working.

Besides Mr. Foote, we had a Mr. Douglas here as veterinary surgeon, living in Doyle Road. When he had left the island, Mr. Burton came and resided at Summerland, Les Gravées. Mr. Brady, constructor of the tramway, had lived there, but moved to a house that used to stand inside the corner of the road behind Les Préaux, St. Martin's.

A most successful teacher of her language was Madame Isemonger, a French-Canadian lady whose husband was the Bailiff's clerk. Their daughter was hardly less renowned as a pianoforte professor. Mr. Julius Arscott, F.C.O., a tall, stoutly-built man, from whom she got her training, was, like his son Father Arscott and other members of the family, a very talented musician.

I must have been nearly twenty ere the use of furze for heating bakers' ovens was generally discarded. Its usage lingered here and there and many sought a baker who still clung to furze, bread baked with it having, in their opinion, and perhaps rightly, a nicer flavour. In earlier years, it was a common thing to see a cart laden with this fuel drawn up before a baker's door.

Few of us remember the old drays used by the London (now the Guernsey) Brewery. They were long and low vehicles running on two wheels. An iron upright in front of them supported a diamond-shaped panel with the letters

P. and A. (Pale Ale) upon it.

They were, however, a familiar sight until less than fifty years ago.

Wrecks were common on our western coast in winter until 1862, when the Hanois Lighthouse was erected. Disaster, of which I have a curious record, befell a timber-laden vessel among others. On the inner side of a heart-shaped portion (5½ ins. x 5 ins.) of what seems to have been a huge nutshell is inscribed the following information: "A Relic of the *Seawitch* of London, 199 tons, John Henry Freeman, master, from Sierra Leone to London with a cargo of Grecian oak and ground nuts, was totally wrecked near the spot known by the name of the Pulias in Portinfer Bay at Grandes Rocques, the 24th of November, 1842. 8 drowned out of 11."

A second instance was that of a large Brazilian ship which came to grief near the same place during the 'forties also, I believe. My grandfather being very fond of shooting used to leave home early in order to reach Grandes Rocques by daybreak. Arriving a few hours after this wreck had occurred, the old gentleman espied a small tin box lying by the roadside and told my father, who accompanied him, to put it in a place of safety, for he judged it to be connected with the tragedy. A similar box was discovered later by another person who obtained a substantial sum for salving it, the boxes proving to be filled with gold dust.

Wreck of the Dunsinane, 1904

Of associations formed during my early manhood, the Amateur Swimming Club, founded in 1886, was one of the most noticeable.[37] The Messrs. W. and —. Newbury arriving here from Jersey, where a prosperous swimming club was already in existence, enlisted the sympathies of Mr. Emra Holmes, of H.M.'s Customs. With the co-operation of the Messrs. Etor and some others, they called a meeting which had satisfactory results.

Although appealing to a smaller number, the Society of Natural Science should not pass unmentioned. It was founded four years before the Swimming Club. Mr. W. Ambridge Luff, Mr. Sharp, Head Master of the Boys' Secondary School, Mr. Geo. Derrick, Mr. A. Collenette and my father were prime movers in its establishment. Miss Selina Best and the Misses Dawber were among the earliest members.

Through the untiring efforts of Mr. Simmonds, the Manager in Herm for a community of monks, the local branch of St. John's Ambulance was started. With the support of Dr. E. L. Robinson, I think, he finally succeeded in getting public recognition of the advantages likely to accrue. Unless my memory fail me, this was about the year 1880.

In 1887 or '88, the Victoria Cottage Hospital was added to our Institutions. The present handsome building had been erected with funds bequeathed by Mr. Nicholas Carey, who had lived in the lower part of the Rohais. It had been destined to continue the work of St. John's Home for Orphans. So few cases presented themselves, however, that it was afterwards agreed to use it as a hospital. Dr. Robinson again was largely associated with the change, as he had for many years desired such an innovation. No one will deny its usefulness and Mr. Carey would have been the first to approve the new departure.

Let me in conclusion say that Herm, in my early years and youth, was occupied by Col. Fielden. Soon after he had left it – I must then have been twenty – it was taken by two brothers named Maxwell who, with their sister and widowed mother, had come to Guernsey a little time before. They did not very long retain it. Mrs. Maxwell married Col. Orme, commanding the regiment, while her daughter became the wife of Mr. Cassel, a banker, but lived only a few years and was buried at the Foulon.

---

37   Instruction in life-saving was given by Mr. A. E. Mauger and some other members in a building now bearing the title of the Albert Mission Hall, near the East end of Pedvin Street.

Gentlemen's Bathing Places, La Valette

Bathing Places, La Valette

THE BATHING PLACES

The bathing place for men, such as it was, lay a little to the west of the existing pool while I was very young. The former entrance to it is now closed by a hoarding. The "horseshoe" or Public Bathing Place, was built when I was nine or ten and was hailed with great delight, but soon proved to be unable to resist a raging storm. Time after time, great blocks of stone of which the steps were made were found to be dislodged. The wash of water, too, in such a narrow space made bathing hazardous in anything but ordinary weather. It was, notwithstanding, much appreciated and ere long became too crowded. For this reason and from the fact that it was used as a sleeping place at night by wayfarers, who composed themselves to rest upon the bench around the dressing-shed, the Private Bathing Place was undertaken. It was a great advance. Besides being more open, the wall enclosing it made bathing safe in any weather, unless the tide were high. Yet even here, in violent storms, a step or two was now and then removed.

It was a common thing to find, on going to the bathing places when a storm had just occurred, numbers of jelly fish, some of them alive and capable of stinging, on the surface of the water. At sundry times, sharks – probably of an inoffensive species – would be reported to be in the neighbourhood.

Among the frequent and daily bathers were Mr. H. Crousaz; Mr. James Carré, sen., chemist; Messrs. the five brothers Carey de Jersey – I wonder if His Lordship the Bishop of the Falkland Islands[38] sometimes thinks of it – the Messrs. Agnew, of whom there were four or five; three or four of Mr. H. Cumber's sons; Mr. Maillard; Mr. Hartwell; Mr. Richard Arscott; Mons. Chotin; Mr. "Harry" Mauger, the Sheriff's son; Messrs. P. D. François and R. D. Leak who, with Mr. Carré, Mr. Arscott and some others were also winter bathers.

General Hackett's son, a strongly-built young man, was wont, though at the risk of cutting his feet upon the bottom, to pander to our curiosity by diving for a heavy stone and carrying it under water around the bathing pool.

From 7 a.m. to 8.30 a.m. the bathing place was nearly always full.

---

38   Resigned, owing to ill-health, in Jan., 1934.

The attendant was Mr. Audoire whose daughter filled the same office at the Ladies' Bathing Place for very many years. He was an ex-naval man but, like many sailors I have met, did not know how to swim. For the assistance of anyone in difficulties, a long pole with a cross-piece at one end was kept at hand, while a lifebuoy or two was readily accessible. To prevent "that sinking feeling" in the case of those who could not swim, cork belts were provided also.

Men while bathing wore no clothing. Women used their cast-off dresses. Mixed bathing was unheard of and, even with precautions, would hardly have been tolerated, except among members of a family.

Only one bathing pool for women was provided, although bathers were numerous, and many years elapsed before the Ladies' Private Bathing Place was built.

Fatal accidents sometimes occurred at the tunnel further on when we had a change of garrison. Soldiers trying to break into barracks late at night missed their footing with disastrous consequences. Steps were later taken, I believe, to guard against this danger.

Tram, Town Church

THE TRAMWAY

Until I was in my 'teens communication between St. Sampson's and the town was very poor. A lumbering one-horse bus and a few shabby cabs were the only public conveyances. A welcome change was brought about by Mr. Brady, an Irish gentleman, who came here. With permission from the States, he set to work to provide us with a tramway, but encountered considerable difficulties, both of a physical and a financial nature. After laying the line from St. Sampson's to the Salerie, he was, if I remember rightly, forced, for lack of funds, to discontinue the enterprise on his own responsibility, and to attempt to form a Company. This was no easy matter, I believe. Work practically ceased for eighteen months or so, until at last the Guernsey Tramway Co. was got together.

Ahead of the times – for I write of nearly sixty years ago – it was from the first a steam tramway.[39] From Richmond Corner to St. Sampson's it ran along the roadway for several years, and not as now, past Manuelle's quarry. Between the battery at Hougue-à-la-Perre and the martello tower opposite it there was then a rise of six feet in the road and over which the tramcars had to pass. It was amusing and not unexciting to watch the driver turn on steam, the car and engine almost toppling down the other side, much like a toboggan.

The original Company ceased in time to flourish.

With the introduction of bicycles, many erstwhile patrons adopted the newer mode of locomotion, other causes, too, contributing to the decline of the tramway's popularity. It was found advisable to reorganize. A few energetic men, and foremost among them, the late Mr. Stedman, re-cast the undertaking with the title of the "Guernsey Railway Company". Under Mr. Stedman's able management, the tramway was electrified, new and larger cars were introduced, while the service was augmented, continuing much as we have it now.

---

39   And only the second not drawn by horses in the Kingdom – the other was in Scotland, if I remember well. One instance, among several, where Guernsey led the way!

Guernsey Press Shop, Smith Street, 1935

NEWSPAPERS

Besides the *Star*, *La Gazette Officielle*, the *Guernsey Advertiser* and *Clarke's Guernsey News* there were published, until forty years ago, two other newspapers, the *Mail and Telegraph*, three times a week, by Messrs. Mackenzie and Le Patourel, at the offices in Lefebvre Street now used by Mr. Dene, signwriter, and the *Comet*, owned and edited by Mr. Maillard, who issued it on Wednesdays and Saturdays from the house in New Street in which Advocates Carey and Son and Advocate Ridgway at present have their offices.

Mr. Maillard, a man of middle height and broadly built, had been at sea and was brilliantly tattooed, as we found when he came to the bathing place.

The *Guernsey Advertiser*, published every Saturday, had been started about 1870, I think, by Mr. T.M. Bichard for the benefit of those who were unable to read French, the language in which the *Gazette* was printed. It was widely read, its circulation reaching some 3,000 copies, and was remarkable for the clearness of its type, as well as for the good quality of the paper used, features which drew comments from strangers.

The *Star*, property of the late Mrs. Le Lièvre, sen., was formerly published only thrice a week, and at 1½d. It appeared on Tuesdays, Thursdays and Saturdays, the same evenings that the *Mail and Telegraph* was issued and, in my early years, was edited by Mr. Talbot, a big and bony man whose Wellington nose was his most remarkable feature. Mr. Sneath, a tall, slim man with long red beard who married Mrs. Biddlecombe, succeeded him, I think.

The *Star* office at that time was situated opposite the higher window and the side entrance of Leale Ltd.

Clarke's Guernsey News was published every Friday and continued with success for many years. The proprietor issued at 3d. monthly *Clarke's Guernsey Magazine*, a record of island affairs and a collection of interesting items. It became a great favourite and was much regretted when its publication ceased.

Other journalistic efforts were essayed by enterprising individuals, but few were of long duration. At one time, we had a *Morning Herald*, published from an office some doors below the *Star*. Appearing at 7 a.m., I think, and sold at a halfpenny, people bought it on their way to bathe. If I remember rightly, it was followed by the *Moon* (?), another halfpenny sheet, and published by Mr. Toms, a printer in Mill Street, but this, too, waned in time.

Le Bailliage, started by Advocate Theophilus de Mouilpied, was a more successful venture. It was long published for him by Mr. F. B. Guerin of High Street but, later, was issued from Manor Place where it continued some years. It was this gentleman who, in the face of much opposition, instituted the Guernsey Herd Book and many now, I think, remember him with gratitude.

Old Sailing Ship at the Coal Quay

Ships & Harbour

Paddle-steamers belonging to the London and South-Western Railway Co., whose local agent was the late Mr. R. L. Spencer, were the chief means of communication between England and the Islands until I was twelve or fourteen years of age. There were besides, the smaller boats *Aquila*, *Cygnus*, and *Brighton* of the Weymouth and Channel Islands Steamship Co., with the late Mr. Sydney Taudevin as agent. The *Brighton* underwent some alterations, most notable of which was the fixing of a hurricane deck, a year or two before the Great Western Railway Company took over the service to Weymouth.

The *Fannie* and her sister ship *Waverley*, the *Brittany*, which had a very good saloon and was sister ship, I think, to the *Normandy* which had been run into and sank in the Solent during a fog, with the *Southampton*, a boat with a single and very tall funnel, were the earliest of the South-Western vessels which I remember.

There was also, at the time, direct communication with London by sea, the screw-steamer *Staperayder* making fortnightly journeys with cargo. When joined, in later years, by the *Stannington*, this service became a weekly one, inaugurating that continued by the *London Queen*, *Foam Queen*, etc., of the present day

Between Guernsey and Plymouth, for many years, a cutter known as the *Intrepid* was wont to sail. At last, the *Commerce* took her place. This was a wooden screw-steamer, the first and only steamer, I believe, ever built in the Channel Islands. As time went on, she was in turn succeeded by the *Plymouth*, or the *Channel Queen* which was

afterwards lost at Le Grand Havre during a fog. Several Breton onion sellers were aboard her and many lost their lives.

Some time before the *Staperayder* came here, a large three-masted and locally-owned screw-steamer, the *Foyle*, was running to Morlaix and St. Brieuc, in Brittany, once a fortnight. As being the only screw-steamer in our harbour, she was something of a curiosity. Owing, I was told by the late Mr. Stickland, to representations made by the English railways to those in France concerning the carrying of her cargoes, the service had, after some years' successful trading, to be abandoned.

The cutter *Fawn*, owned and commanded by Captain Piprell, sailed regularly, however, to St. Malo every week. Sailings to Binic were made as well by his cutter *Reindeer* until succeeded by the new boat *Echo*. The *Echo* was, however, wrecked in a storm, off L'Etacq, in Jersey, while bringing goods here for the Christmas market, her owner, her commander, Captain Quesnel, her crew and passengers, among them, Mr. Ferguson, poulterer, all perishing. She was replaced by the *Œnone*, if I remember rightly.

I think it was in the "eighties" that a cattle trading schooner named the *I.C.U.* made regular voyages to Corunna, but discontinued them when restrictions on the importation of cattle were imposed. Everyone admired the rapidity with which she made her journeys. Years before, cargoes of Spanish cattle had been landed here and had been the cause of much excitement. An animal got free on one occasion and made for a spectator, whose presence of mind in jumping over the wire rope along the quay, saved him from injury. The wonder is that he was cool enough to avoid falling into the water! A lady near the bathing places came unexpectedly upon a beast that had escaped, another time, but scared it off by opening her umbrella in its face.

In my childhood, a very pretty, but said to be unseaworthy, paddle-steamer, *Queen of the Isles*, owned and commanded by Captain Scott, used to run to Alderney and Cherbourg. As an illustration, I have heard my elders say that once she lay on her beam ends when coming from Cherbourg, all on board wondering if she would be righted.

The *Princess*, another paddle-steamer, followed and was not replaced for several years until the *Courier*, an excellent screw-steamer, no bigger than herself, succeeded her, doing duty until recent years.

Nor must I, in my remarks, forget the steamers of the Guernsey Towing Co., for they played a large part in the simple pleasures of those days, besides offering their services to the many sailing ships – chiefly colliers

Paddle-steamer, Rescue

– that used to come to Guernsey. Discharging their cargoes at St. Peter Port, they were afterwards towed to St. Sampson's to load with stone for the repair of London's streets.

The *Rescue*, a smart little clinker-built paddle-boat, painted green and white, was the earliest of the tugs that I remember, with the *Gosforth*, an inferior boat, for her companion. This latter vessel, springing a leak, was afterwards lost in calm weather, between Herm and Jethou when bringing the Rev. William Collings, Seigneur of Sark, and his belongings to Guernsey. Fortunately, no one perished.

While the Alderney steamer made trips to Sark every Monday in summer at two francs a head, with a charge of fivepence by the boatmen there for landing, the *Rescue* went to Herm for one franc each, the boat for Sark in those days starting at 9.30, half an hour before the boat to Herm, because of the greater distance. Some years afterwards, the tug began to take excursionists to Sark on Thursdays, besides continuing her Monday trip to Herm.

The *Rescue* was succeeded by another of the name, a round-seamed boat of greater size and speed, but still a paddle. A screw-steamer, the *Alert*, capable of steaming twelve knots an hour, was a later acquisition and was running with the *Rescue* for a few years. Captains Lihou and Bichard were the commanders of these steamers, Captain Lihou having "come to the *Rescue*(s)" from the beginning, and changing to the *Alert* on her arrival.

Paddle-steamer, Alert, in Sark

The first *Rescue* had salved, about the year 1873, a large three-masted Norwegian or Swedish timber-laden vessel called the *Scandinav* that had overturned off our West coast during rough weather. Her masts, dragging on the bottom here and there, had proved a difficulty, but it was overcome and I remember seeing, as a boy, the upturned hulk lying between the pierheads until it was safely brought to the mouth of the Careening Hard. £1,100 was paid in salvage money, I have heard. Two other vessels, but of somewhat smaller size, were recovered under similar circumstances by their boats ere this once prosperous Company became defunct, owing to the increasing number of steam colliers and to the advent of a rival in the *Assistance*, a powerful tug of the English type, with screw propeller.

As a young man, I had often with my father availed myself of the 1/- marine trips made, for a few summers, to the bays, the back of Herm, or around Sark, by the second *Rescue* and the *Alert* starting at 6 p.m., we spent about two hours on the water.

In advertisements of the

EXCURSIONS
PER STEAMERS
'ALERT' & 'RESCUE'

DURING the MONTH of OCTOBER one of the above Steamers will weather permitting, leave St. Peter-Port Harbour for

SARK—Every TUESDAY at 9.30 a.m.
Every THURSDAY at 9.30 a.m.
Every SATURDAY at 11 a.m.
FARE.....................2/- British.

HERM.—Every MONDAY at 10 a.m.
Every WEDNESDAY at 1.30 p.m.
Every FRIDAY at 1.30 p.m.
FARE.....................1/3

J. T. LAINÉ, Manager.

movements of the steamers of those days, most of them were "favourite" and, no matter what their knottage, all were "fast and powerful" !

In 1873 or '4, the South-Western Railway Co. added to their fleet the sister ships *Guernsey* and *South-Western* (?), often employing them on this route, especially, I think, in winter, when the service to the Islands was curtailed. The *Waverley* had been lost on the Platte Boue in a fog some time before, while the *Havre*, a smaller vessel had met with the same fate, and on the same spot, the following season. The *Southampton* was removed and, later on, the *Brittany*, the *Fannie* only remaining with the *Diana*, a screw-steamer which had replaced the *Southampton* and had become a favourite with passengers, until the *Hilda* and the *Ella* were placed upon this station.

Before the building of the ill-fated *Stella*, wrecked in 1899, and her sister ships *Lydia* and *Frederica*, a screw-steamer called the *Dora* was added to the other boats. Great speed had been expected of her, but she proved a disappointment.

I should like to record here that, to the best of my belief, the late Mr. Wm. Fuzzey and his brother, Mr. Fred, were instrumental in obtaining the greater security for passengers to be found on our mail-boats today. The recurring disasters to the steamers when we were all young men could not fail to arouse attention, nor to give cause for grave concern. Engaged in cabinet making and accustomed to the sea, these gentlemen urged that rafts should be constructed which, lashed only to the deck, might quickly be cut

Stella entering St Peter Port harbour

free. They proposed, I think, that a chest for mails with seats fixed to it be set up in the centre, rendering the rafts useful at all times as well as a safeguard in emergency. I am under the impression that the firm of I. C. Fuzzey was commissioned to make a few.

The Great Western Railway Co. had, some months earlier, taken over the service to Weymouth, their screw-steamers *Lynx*, *Gazelle* and *Antelope* soon becoming very popular, owing to the speed at which they travelled and to the excellent catering on board.

I have known these little vessels to come from Jersey, under forced draught – a means by which the fires are made to burn more fiercely – in an hour and seventeen minutes, on more than one occasion.

Hand cranes were in general use for unloading the sailing ships and were invariably employed for landing horned cattle, which was by means of a very broad canvas sling passed under their belly. One of the steam cranes, the "elephant", ran on broad wheels and travelled along the harbour when required.

Conspicuous among the pleasure craft of my early years and youth was a pretty little steam launch owned by Mr. St. John Gore and named the *Erin*. She was lengthened, later on, by several feet, yet it seemed to me that what she may have gained in comfort she had lost in beauty. Near her in the Pool lay moored a sailing boat belonging to Mr. William Jones of "Chez Nous", while the brothers Carrington, engaged at the time in the Old Bank,

Pleasure craft moored in St Peter Port harbour

Mailboat entering the Harbour

had another. A third was owned by Mr. Charles Biddlecombe, nephew of Mr. James Gardner of the Royal Hotel. The *Prima Donna* was the name of Mr. Herbert "Dappy" Arscott's sailing boat, and there were several others. Mr. Thomas Martel, jun., kept his in the "Wet" Dock, so-called, until quite recent years, because of the original design to enclose it with gates.

Boats for hire could be obtained from Mr. "Ted" Williams and from Mr. Wm. Berryman, both of whom kept watch for customers near the Albert Statue. The *Anonyma* was Mr. Williams' sailing boat which, with the two-oared rowing boats, *Sylf*, *Non Pareil*, *Daisy*, etc., was often in demand. The *May*, *Princess* and other rowing boats belonged to Mr. Berryman, as well as a stiff sailing boat, the *Swallow*. The rowing boats were let out at one franc an hour and the sailing boats at 1/3.

The Harbour Master of the time was Captain Abm. Martin, father, by his second wife, of the Messrs. Martin Bros. Captain Martin "looked his part" among the States officials. Though not particularly tall, he was a very stout man, and yet would briskly walk along the harbour, Malacca walking-stick in hand and swinging both his arms, the gold watch-chain across his breast, the gilt buttons of his uniform, and gold band around his cap enhancing his appearance.

A genial successor to Captain Martin was Captain W. Jones of Candie Road. Less stout than Captain Martin, he was much of the same build.

Landing at Guernsey

The "refreshment room" was Mrs. Pierce, or Pearse's "coffee house", a large wooden shed having for floor the granite setts with which the quays were paved, and standing above No.1 landing stage. Charges were small and patronage was great.

A wooden hoarding for many years enclosed St. Julian's Emplacement and stone in heaps was kept inside it. Buildings which, from their tarry covering, became known as the "Black Sheds" were afterwards erected but were most unsightly and were none too soon replaced by the present ones of granite.

The original North arm of the Old Harbour remained until, perhaps, twenty years ago. At high spring tides the middle of its quay, which sloped from the pierhead, was four feet under water

Yachts, both sailing[40] and steam yachts, were, in my youth, quite "common objects of the seashore", their owners spending a lot of money in our town on wines and spirits, tobacco and cigars, as well as on fruit and lobsters. Twelve or fourteen yachts of varying size at anchor in the Pool was no unusual sight, and once, I counted twenty-two.

Employed at the South-Western office, now forming the northern end of Messrs. G. Momo and Co's, were tall Mr. Tardif who lived at "Osmington",

---

40   The *Boadicea*, said to have taller masts than any other yacht, and, I think, the *Guinevere*, among them.

St. Martin's; Mr. Bichard, a much smaller man and brother of the publisher, with others. Mr. Guilbert and Mr. Washington had to do with the arrival of the steamers. Besides Mr. S. Taudevin, the agent, Mr. Fred. Robin, now an "ancient mariner", is the only one that I can think of in connection with the Weymouth boats.

The boats to Weymouth, in those days, left Jersey[41] in the evening. Starting at 5 o'clock, they arrived here at 7.30. On calm evenings I have often heard, when fishing from a boat, their paddles strike the water, though the ship herself was fully an hour's distance from our harbour.

To guard the local fisheries, we had a little paddle boat, *H.M.S. Dasher*, stationed at Jersey.

In conclusion, I may add that, while still a child, I witnessed the departure for China of Mr. Edward Carrington's *Morning Star* (?). The last of Guernsey's foreign-going sailing ships, she was making her last voyage and had been here about three weeks refitting ere she made her start from near the Careening Hard.

Since writing the above, I have been told that there was yet a later, though smaller, vessel, the *Mary Ann*, the captain of which is still living at St. Sampson's.

---

41   A small steamer named *Griffin*, which I think had been a yacht, used, 60 years ago, to ply between Jersey and France. She belonged to the South-Western Railway Co.

Albert Dock, St Peter Port Harbour

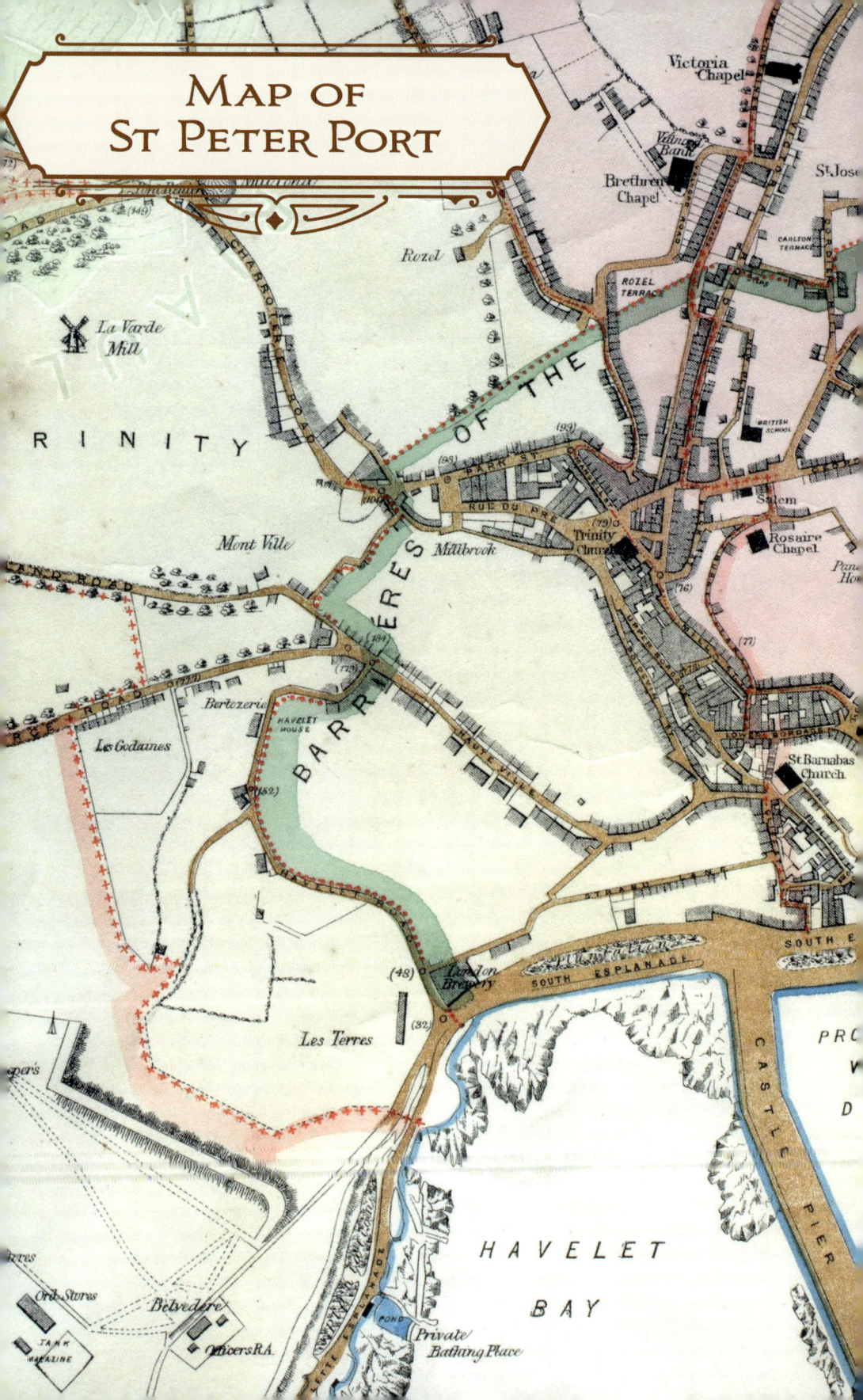

Map of St Peter Port

LIST OF ILLUSTRATIONS

Page	Subject	Source
4	G.W.J.L Hugo	Hugo
6	S.G.Hugo	Guernsey Almanack 1867, PL
9	Hugo Family, 1906	Hugo
9	Hugo Family at Petit Bot, 1920s	Hugo
10	Cobbled Street	CTC, © PL
12	Smith Street	Postcard, Foote
13	Mrs Le Lacheur	Griggs Almanack 1880, PL
14	Hartwell's Piano Store	Guernsey Illustrated, PL
15	Smith Street	Postcard, PL
16	High Street	Postcard, Foote
18	Abraham Bishop	Postcard, PL
19	Torode & Nicolle	Griggs Almanack, 1882, PL
20	Old Bank House	Le Lievre's Almanack, 1880, PL
21	Le Grand Carrefour	CTC, © PL
22	Pollet	Postcard, Foote
24	Arthur Maunder	Burnside, PL
25	Pollet	Postcard, PL
26	Market Square	CTC, © PL
28	Commercial Arcade	PL
29	Market Steps	Postcard, Foote
30	Guille-Alles Library	CTC, © PL
31	French Halles	Postcard, Foote
32	John De La Mare	Hill's Directory, 1874, Foote
34	Town Church	Postcard, Foote
35	Bucktrout's	CTC, © PL
36	Fountain Street	CTC, © PL
39	Le Bordage	CTC, © PL
41	Mrs. Nicolle's Shop	CTC, © PL
42	H. Turner	Le Lievre's Almanack, 1884, PL
42	Maison Le Noury	CTC, © PL
44	B. Symes	Guerin's Almanack, 1899, PL
45	Mansell Court	CTC, © PL
46	Marmain's Stores	GMAG
47	Keiller's Factory	T. Singleton, CTC, © PL
48	JS Saunders, Trinity Sq.	PL
48	Lovell & Cox advertisement	*The Star*, PL
50	Vauvert	Postcard, PL
51	Bordage	Postcard, PL
52	St Julian's Avenue	Postcard, Foote
53	Gardner's Royal Hotel	Postcard, Foote
54	Mrs. Margaret Neve	M A Neve, PL
55	Rouge Huis House	Postcard, PL
56	Ivy Gates	CTC, © PL
57	Auld Funeral, The Grange	CTC, © PL
58	Rev Carey Brock	Notable People file, PL
58	Rev Thomas Bell	Notable People file, PL

Page	Subject	Source
58	Rev Nassau Cathcart	Guernsey Gossip, 1908, PL
58	Canon Foran	Guernsey Gossip, 1907, PL
61	Sir Peter Stafford Carey	Oil painting by Frank Brooks, Royal Court
61	Victor Hugo	Postcard, PL
61	Dr. Benjamin Collenette	Shaw, *Methodist New Connexion*, 1910, PL
61	Col. William Bell	Notable People file, PL
62	Meeting the Boat	Postcard, Foote
62	Bandstand, Candie Grounds	Postcard, Foote
64	Tom Thumb wedding	Wikipedia
65	St Julian's Hall	T. Singleton, CTC, © PL
65	Two-Headed Nightingale	Wikipedia
66	Royal Milita sergeant	F.W. Guerin, CTC, © PL
67	Boudelot procession	CTC, © PL
68	Fire Engine	CTC, © PL
68	Fire Fighting, Coal Quay	CTC, © PL
70	Gas Lamp, Commercial Arcade	Postcard, PL
70	Jack Trump, Town Crier	F.W. Guerin, CTC, © PL
71	Excursion Car	CTC, © PL
72	In the Fish Market	Postcard, Foote
73	Grape Thinners	CTC, © PL
74	Ropewalk, St. John's	CTC, © PL
75	Mr. Foote, veterinary surgeon	Foote
76	Wreck of *Dunsinane*	F.W. Guerin, PL
78	Bathing Places	Postcard, Foote
78	La Vallette	Postcard, Foote
80	Tram, Town Church	CTC, © PL
82	Newspapers	Newspaper collection, PL
82	Guernsey Press Shop	CTC, © PL
84	*Le Baillage*	Newspaper collection, PL
84	Sailing Ship, Coal Quay	CTC, © PL
85	*Staperayder* advertisement	Newspaper collection, PL
87	Paddle Steamer *Rescue*	PL
88	*Alert* in Sark	PL
88	Excursions advertisement	Newspaper collection, PL
89	*Stella* arriving in harbour	PL
90	Harbour	Postcard, Foote
91	Mailboat entering harbour	Postcard, Foote
92	Landing at Guernsey	Postcard, Foote
93	Albert Dock	Postcard, Foote
94-5	Map of St Peter Port, 1873	Map Collection, PL

(*Plan of the Town and Parish of St Peter Port Guernsey*. Surveyed and drawn by James Duquemin, surveyor to the States of Guernsey. Published for the Proprietor by F. Clarke, States Arcade, Guernsey, 1873)

Abbreviations

PL	Priaulx Library
CTC	Carel Toms Collection
GMAG	Guernsey Museum & Art Gallery
Hugo	Hugo Family collection
Foote	Foote Family collection
Wikipedia	Wikipedia (Creative Commons Licence)

INDEX

A

Abraham, Mrs. 31
actors 30, 38
Adam, Mr. 44
agents 39, 85, 93
Agnew, Messrs. 79
Agnew, Mr. 39
Agnew, Mr. Alfred 17, 19
Agnew, Mr. R.C. 17
Agnew, Mr. T. H. 38
Ahier, Mr. 33
Albert House 17
Albert Mission Hall 77
Albert Statue 91
Alderney 86, 87
Alert (ship) 87, 88
Allen, Mr. 27
Allès, Mr. 32
Allez, Mr. 27, 28
Allez, Mr. Bredthaft 27
Allez Street 7, 8, 51, 69
All Saints' Church 53
Amateur Swimming Club 77
Amherst Road 54
Amies, Mr. 39
Amy, Mr. 39, 40
Amy, Mrs. 39
Anderson, Mr. 49
Anderson's 37
André, Mons. 23, 53
Angel, Mrs 14
Angel, Mr. T. 50
Ann's Place 71
Anonyma (ship) 91
Antelope (ship) 90
Aquila (ship) 05
Arcadia (house) 28
architects 38
Arnold, Mr. 27, 70
Arscott, Father 75
Arscott, Mr. 17, 69, 79

Arscott, Mr. Herbert 91
Arscott, Mr. Julius, F.C.O. 75
Arscott, Mr. Richard 17, 79
Artizans' Institute 32
art pottery dealers 27
Assembly Rooms 32, 64
Assistance (ship) 67, 88
attendant, bathing places 80
Aubert and Ozanne 50
Aubert, Dan 50
Aubert, Mme. 50
Aubert, Mr. 50
Aubert, Mr. D. 50
Aubert, Mr. James 50, 51
Aubert, Mr. sen. 50
auctions 40
Audoire, Mr. 80
Austin, Mrs. W. J. 31
authoress 18

B

baby linen warehouse 28
Bachmann, Messrs & Co 18, 21
Back Street 33
Bagnall, Mr. 63
Bailiff's clerk 75
Bailiff's Cross Road 57
Baker, Mrs. George 46
bakers 13, 23, 37, 38, 39, 40, 44, 45, 46,
    49, 50, 75
bands, military 63, 65
bandstand 63
Bang, Mrs. 53
bankers 77
Banks' (bookshop) 21
Barbet, Miss M.A. 14
Barbet, Mr. J. 72
Barbet, Mr. James 17, 20
Barbet, Mr. Stephen 14, 20
Barclay's Bank 38
Bartlett, Mr. 45

basket business 31
basket trap 59
Bath chairs 71
bathing 63
Bathing Places 5, 39, 78, 79
Battery 53
Baxter, Mrs. 32
bazaars 32, 64
Béghin, Mme I 17
Béghin, Mr. E. 20
Bell, Colonel Wm. 59, 61
Belle of St. Saviour's (comedy) 64
bell-hangers 50
Bell, Rev. T. 58, 59
Belmont (house) 59
Bennett, Mr. 29
Bernays, Professor Albert J. 69
Berryman, Mr. Wm. 91
Best, Miss Selina 77
Best, Mr. S. 5, 31, 73
Bichard, Captain 87
Bichard, Mr. 93
Bichard, Mr. T.M. 83
bicycles 24, 29, 63, 81
Biddlecombe, Mr. Charles 91
Biddlecombe, Mrs. 38, 83
Bidmead, Mr. 19, 21, 60
Binic, Brittany 86
Bird, Mr. 70
Bishop, Mr. Abraham 18, 19
Bishop, Mr. Stephen 19, 66
Bishop of the Falkland Islands 79
Black, Mr. 28
blacksmiths 48
Blake, Mr. A. 24, 29
Blicq, Mr. sen. 40
Boadicea (yacht) 92
boating 63
boats for hire 91
boats, toy 18
bookbinders 15, 43
bookshops 14, 20, 27, 29
bootmakers 13, 17, 29, 34, 41, 43
Boots 21
boot shops 17, 20, 37, 43, 74
Bordage 11, 32, 38–39, 46, 51, 73
Bosq Lane 63
boudelot 66, 67
Bouillonne Steps 49
Box and Cox 64

box-cart 73
Brady, Mr. 75, 81
Bramwell, Mr. 71
Brand, Mr. G. 30
bread 75
Brehaut, Mr. 19
Brehaut, Rev. 56
Brennan, Mr. 50
Brennan, Mrs 13
Breton 31, 86
Brewery, London 75
Brighton (ship) 85
Bristol 19
British Bakery 39, 40
britskas 71
Brittany, France 86, 89
Brittany (ship) 85
Brock, Mr. W. 59
Brock, Rev. Thos. 59
Brock Road 38, 54, 55, 56, 71
Brock Road Chapel 38
Brock, Sir Isaac 21
Brock, Very Rev. Carey 58, 59
Brouard, Mr. 27, 37
Brouard, Mr. Abraham 27
broughams 71
Bucktrout, Messrs. and Co. 5, 32, 33, 35, 38
Bucktrout, Mr. 38
builders 37, 51
bullock carts 73
Burnt Lane 43, 50, 54
Burnt Lane Steps 43
Burr, Mrs. 27
Burton, Mr. 75
Burwood Mr. J. 20
buses 55, 81
Bush, Mr. 45
butchers 31
Butten, Sergeant 64

C

cabinet makers 23, 46, 49, 50, 54, 74, 89
cabs 81
Cadic, Mr. Eugene 66
Cadic, Mr. Wm. 33, 38
Caines, Mr. 40
Cambridge Hotel 54
Cambridge Park 6, 54, 63, 66

Canada 38
Candie Grounds 53, 62, 69
Candie Library 60
Candie Road 51, 53, 91
candlemakers 33
Cannon, Mr. 40
Capital and Counties Bank 21
Carey and Son, Advocates 83
Carey, Colonel de Vic 59
Carey, Dr. Francis 59
Carey, Miss 54
Carey, Mr. Julius 59
Carey, Mr. Nicholas 77
Carey, Mrs. 59
Carey, Sir Godfrey 59, 60
Carey, Sir Peter Stafford 8, 39, 60, 61
carpenters 51, 74
carpet makers 74
carpets 15, 32
Carré and Nephew 20
Carré, Messrs. Jno. and T. 20
Carré, Mr. 79
Carré, Mr. James sen. 32, 40, 79
carriages 59, 63, 71
Carrington brothers 90
Carrington, Mr. Edward 93
cars 72, 81
carts 75
carvers 18, 40, 44, 49
Cassel, Mr. 77
Castle Cornet 62
Câtel Church 33
Cathcart, Rev. Nassau 58, 59
cattle, importation of 86, 90
Channel Islands Hotel 54
Channel Islands Steamship Co. 85
Channel Queen (ship) 85
charcuterie 34, 40
Charroterie 20
Charroterie Mills 40, 45
charwomen 74
cheesemongers 18, 28
chemists 15, 20, 21, 23, 27, 32, 33, 37, 40,
     43, 44, 45, 49, 79
Cherbourg, Normandy 80
Chez Nous (house) 90
chimney-sweeps 51
China 93
china shops 17
Chotin, Mons. 21, 79

Christmas 65, 72, 86
Churches
     All Saints Church 53
     Brock Road Chapel 38
     Castel Church 33
     Holy Trinity Church 45, 59
     Parish Church, St Peter Port 59
     Salem Chapel 59
     Salvation Army 59
     St. James's Church 59
     St. John's Church 59
     St. Joseph's Church 59
     St. Paul's Church 73
     St. Peter-in-the-Wood Church 59
     St. Sampson's Church 59
     Vale Church 59
Church Hill 10
Church Square 34
cigars 19, 92
Clameur de Haro 73
Clarence Hotel 54
Clarke, Mr. Frederick sen. 33
Clarke's Guernsey Magazine 83
Clarke's Guernsey News 83
Clifton Hall 64, 65
Clifton Steps 27, 32
Clothier, Mr. 37
clothing shops 17
Clouting, Mrs. 44
cloves, cure for colds 60
Cluett, Mr. J. 38
Cluett, Mr. T. W. 37
Coal Quay 84
Cobo 56
coffee houses 92
Cohen, Mr. R. 20
Cohu, Mr. 19
Cohu, Mr. Elisha M. 60
Colborne Road 73
Coles' Hotel 54
College Street 71
Collenette, Dr. B. 24, 59, 61
Collenette, Mr. A. 27, 64, 77
Collenette, Mr. B 13
colliers 88
Collings, Dr. 54
Collings, Joseph 20
Collings, Miss Ellen 59
Collings, Mr. Alfred 59
Collings, Mr. J.B. 20

Collings, Mr. Joseph 59
Collings, Rev. W. 59, 87
Collins, Mr. 24
Collivet, Mme. Rose 31, 71
Comet, The (newspaper) 82, 83
Commerce (ship) 85
Commercial Arcade 11, 18, 26–33, 40, 50, 69, 70, 72
    Central Passage 28, 32
Commercial Bank 20
commercial travellers 54
confectioners 37, 44, 49
Connaught House 54
Connellan, Dr. 24
Constables 59, 60
Constables' Office 33
Constantin, Dr. O. 23
Constantin, Mons. L. 23
Constitution Steps 32
Contrée Mansell 27, 42, 44, 45
coopers 33, 74
Corbin, Dr. M. A. B. 59
Cornet Street 5, 23, 33, 35, 38, 69
Cornwall 7, 51
Coronation Road 54
Corunna, Spain 86
costume business 17, 19
Courier (ship) 86
Courtenay, Mr. W. 43
Court House 53, 64
court usher 31
Cowley, Mr. 41
Cox. *See* Lovell and Cox
Cox, Mr. 27, 29
Cox, Mr. sen. 72
Crane, Rev. 50
cranes 90
Creasey & Son 5, 19
Cressard, Mr. J. 23
cricket 63
crinolines 71
Crocodile (ship) 67
Crousaz, Jurat 17
Crousaz, Mr. H. 21, 33, 72, 79
Crousaz, Mr. W. 17, 72
Cuell, Mr. 53
Cumber, Mr. 23
Cumber, Mr. H. 23, 37, 79
Cumber, Mr, junior 23
cutters 37, 85, 86

Cygnus (ship) 85

D

Daddo, Mrs. 28
Daisy (boat) 91
Dalgairns Road 55, 69
Davey, Mr. John 71
Davies, Mr. 43
Dawber, Misses 77
Day, Mr. 44
Dean of Guernsey 58, 59
De Bertrand's 37
de Carteret, Mr. 19
decorators 14, 43
de Garis, Mr. 38
de Guérin, Mr. E. T. 40
de Jersey, Mr. 37
de Jersey, Mr. Wm. 60
de la Cour, Mrs. 31
de la Mare, Messrs. and Co 38, 43
de la Mare, Mr. 32
de la Mare, Mr. Chas. Gruchy 32
de Lancey, Miss 59
de la Rue 37
de la Rue, Mr. 33
de Mouilpied, Advocate Theophilus 84
de Mouilpied, Mr. Jno. 50
Dene, Mr. 83
dentists 7
Deputy Sergeant 60
Derrick, Mr. 33
Derrick, Mr. Geo. 77
de Sausmarez, Captain Philip 59
de Sausmarez family of St. Martins 13
detective, private 43
Devenish and Co 39
Diana (ship) 89
Dobie, Dr. 24
Dora (ship) 89
Douglas, Mr. 75
Doyle House 54
Doyle Road 54, 75
Draper, Mr. sen. 45
drapers 15, 17, 18, 19, 20, 21, 27, 28, 38, 43, 44
drays, brewery 75
Dubras 17
Dubras, Mons. 39
Dumaresq, Mr. 50

Dumont, Mme. 31
Dunsinane (ship) 74
Duplain, Miss 13
Dupuy, Mr. Edgar 27
Dupuy, Mr. Edwin Winter 20, 27
Duquemin, Mr. 24
Durant's, Mrs 13
dust carts 71
dwarfs 64
dyers 37, 50

E

eating-houses 37
Echo (ship) 86
écrivains 14, 20, 27, 33
Edgeborough (house) 55
eggs 31
Elizabeth College 63
Elizabeth College, principal of 59
Ella (ship) 89
Elm Grove 54
England 34, 43, 45, 63, 72, 85
Erin (boat) 90
Espérance (house) 55
Etor, Messrs. 77
excursion cars 71
excursions to the bays 63
Exeter, Devon 7
exhibitions 64

F

Fannie (ship) 85, 89
Farquharson, Misses 59
Fawn (ship) 86
Feock, Cornwall 7
Ferguson, Miss 20
Ferguson, Mr. 24, 86
Ferguson, Mr. and Mrs. 31
Ferguson, Mr. N. 24
Feuillerat, Mme. 45
Feuillerat, Mons. 44
Feuillerat, Mons. and Mme. G. 43, 44
fichu (Guernsey bonnet) 79
Fielden, Col. 77
Field, Mr. 13
firefighting 8, 68, 69
firelighters 69
fireworks 43, 66

fisheries 93
Fisheries, The 31
Fisher, Mr. 43
fishing 18, 93
Fish Market 32, 36, 37, 72
fishmongers 30
Flambe, Mr. 60
Fleure, Mr. 44
florists 43
Foam Queen (ship) 85
football 63
Foote, Mr. 75
forage dealers 49
Foran, Very Rev. William Canon 58, 59
Fort George 69
Forward, Mr. 46
Fosse Landry 55, 74
Foulon Cemetery 77
Foulon Vale 56
Fountain Street 10, 32, 34, 36–38
Fox, Mr. 40
Foyle (ship) 86
France 31, 86, 93
François, Mons. P.D. 24, 79
Frederica (ship) 89
Freeman, John Henry 76
French Halles 30, 31
fruit 31, 33, 72, 92
fruiterers 30
fuel 75
furniture dealers 23, 40, 43, 46, 49
furriers 17, 27
furze ovens 75
Fuzzey, Mr. F.G. 19, 89
Fuzzey, Mr. I.C. 32, 46, 90
Fuzzey, Mr. Wm. 89
Fuzzey's, Messrs. 5, 46

G

gâche 50
Gale, Mr. 74
Gallienne, Mr. James 60
Gallienne, Rev. M. sen. 60
game dealers 30
gardeners 74
Gardner, James 23, 38, 91
Gardner, Mr. 44, 45, 53, 55
Garnier, Mons. Arséne 53
Gas Company 70

gasfitters 29, 44
Gaudin's 14
Gaved, Miss 29
Gazelle (ship) 90
Gazette Officielle (newspaper) 37, 82, 83
general merchants 39
Genêt, Mons. 49
Gibson, Mr. 30
gigs 59
Gilbert and Sullivan 65
gilders 18, 49
Gillet, Mme 17
ginger beer 63
Gladstone House 56
glass dealers 27
Gliddon, Mr. 39
Goesle, Mr. 37
Golden Lion (public house) 31, 32
Good Friday 66
goose, wild. *See* ouaie sauvage
Gore, Mr. St. John 90
Gosforth (boat) 87
Government House Hotel 54
Government Secretary 59, 61
Grace, Misses 18
Grandes Rocques 76
Grand Havre 86
Grange 51, 54, 55, 56, 57, 59
Grange End (house) 55
Grange Villa (house) 59
grapes, exportation of 6, 72–73
Great Western Railway Co. 85, 90
greengrocers 44
Green, Miss 18
Green, Mrs. 33
Greffier 60
Greffier, Deputy 60
Griffin (ship) 93
Grigg, Miss 20
Grigg, Mr. Thomas 18
grindery 32, 43
grocers 13, 17, 23, 27, 28, 32, 37, 38, 39,
    43, 46, 49, 53
ground nuts 76
Grove End (house) 54
Gruchy, Mr. 32
Grut, Mr. 5, 23, 38
Grut, Mr. A. 49, 72
Grut, Mr. Norman 23
Grut, Mr. T.A. 23, 38

guano 39
Guerin, Mr. F.B. 20, 84
Guernésiais 27, 33, 72
Guernier, Mme. 40
Guernsey Advertiser (newspaper) 37, 82, 83
Guernsey Brewery. *See* London Brewery
Guernsey-French. *See* Guernésiais
Guernsey Gaslight Company 14
Guernsey Herd Book 84
Guernsey Press (newspaper) 64, 82
Guernsey Railway Co. 81
Guernsey (ship) 89
Guernsey Towing Co. 86
Guernsey Tramway Co. 81
Guidez, Rev. Amadeus 59
Guilbert, Mr. 93
Guille-Allès Library 29, 30, 32, 33, 60, 64
Guille, Mr. 29, 30, 32, 33
Guinevere (yacht) 92
gunsmiths 40

H

haberdashers 24
Hackett, General 79
hairdressers 15, 17, 21, 29, 39, 40, 44, 46
Haize, Mr. 34
Hall, Mr. 51
Hambley, Mr. 54
Hambling, Mr. 54
Hamel, Mr. sen. 38
Hamilton, Mr. 17
Hamson, Mr. 53
Handy Shop, The 45
Hanois Lighthouse 76
Hansford, Mr. 51
Harbour, St Peter Port 53, 63, 66, 67, 70,
    72, 85–93, 86
    Black Sheds 92
    Careening Hard 88, 93
    Harbour Master 91
    No.1 landing stage 92
    Old Harbour 92
    pierheads 88, 92
    Pool, The 90, 92
    quays 92
    St. Julian's Emplacement 92
    Wet Dock 91
Harbour, St. Sampson's 87
Harcourt, Fred 43

Harp and Crown (public house) 31
Harris, Mr. T. 40
Hartwell and Woodward (shop) 15
Hartwell, Mr. 14, 15, 79
Harvey, General 54
hatters 30, 32
Hauteville 20, 40, 59
Havre (ship) 89
Hawke, Mr. 45
Head, Mr. 40
Henry, Miss 17, 49
Henry's gâche shop 29
Herm 6, 63, 72, 77, 87, 88
Heuzé, Mme. 37
Hickey, Mr. M. 38
Hicks. *See* Targett and Hicks
Hicks, Mr. 51
Highlands Hotel 54
High Street 16–21, 24, 27, 32, 37, 50, 69, 72, 74, 84
Hilda (ship) 89
Hillman Ltd 46
Hill's (shop) 44
Himalaya (ship) 67
Hirzel Street 53
Hitchins, Messrs. and Son 23
H.M. Comptroller 60
H.M. Customs 77
H.M. Procureur 60
H.M.'s A.D.C. 59
H.M.S. Dasher (boat) 93
hoarding 53, 79, 92
Hodder, Mr. 30
Holmes, Mr. Emra 77
Holy Trinity Church 45, 59
Hooper, Mr. F. 71
Horn Street 38
horses 11, 81
hosiers 32
Hospital, Victoria Cottage 77
Hotels
    Cambridge Hotel 53, 54
    Channel Islands Hotel 53
    Clarence Hotel 38
    Coles' Hotel 32, 37
    Government House Hotel 53
    Highlands Hotel 54
    Market Hotel 32
    Queen's Hotel 23, 24
    Royal Hotel 23, 53, 91
    Victoria Hotel 18
    Yacht Hotel 21
Hougue-à-la-Perre 81
house furnishers 50
Hugo, Marie-Madeleine (née Guérin) (author's wife) 7, 9
Hugo, Samuel (author's grandfather) 7, 76
Hugo, Samuel George (author's father) 6, 7, 20, 32, 33, 50, 76, 77, 88
Hugo, Thomas Henry (author's son) 7
Hugo, Victor (no relation) 6, 60, 61
Hunkin, Mr. 27
Hutchisson, Fred 20
Hutton, Mr. 51

I

I.C.U. (ship) 86
Ingrouille, Mr. J. H. 40
Irish, Mrs. 31
ironmongers 17, 37, 49, 50
Isabelle Road 56
Isemonger, Madame 75
Ivy Gates 56

J

Jackson, Mr. 28
Jago, Mrs. 27
Jamouneau, Mr. Wm. 43
Javelot, Madame 23
jellyfish 79
Jersey 7, 34, 63, 66, 71, 77, 86, 90, 93
Jethou 87
jeweller 21, 23, 27, 28, 43, 46
Jones, Captain W. 91
Jones, Macey 20
Jones, Mr. William 90
Jory, Mr. 34, 69
Jubilee House 69

K

Kaines, Mr. 40
Keiller, Messrs. James and Sons 24, 33, 45, 47
Kennedy, Rev. J. Doyle 59
Keppel Place 56
Kitts, Mr. Charles 13

L

La Brasserie (house) 39
Lacombe, Mme. 28, 72
Lacombe, Mons. 28, 29
La Gibauderie 55, 69
La Hauteur 74
Lainé, Mr. E. 20
Lainé, Mr. John T. 17
Lakes, Rev. J. 59
Lamb, Mr. 27
lamplighters 70
lamp, public gas 70
landaus 71
Lane-Clarke, Mrs. 59
Langlois, Miss 44
La Plaiderie 24, 59
La Porte Vase 50
La Rue aux Prêtres 53
La Salerie 53
La Serre, Mr. C. 59
La Tourgand 23
Lauga, Mr. 60
Lausanne, Switzerland 17
La Valette 78. *See also* Bathing Places
Laventure, Mr. 44
Leadenheall Market. *See* French Halles
Leak, Mr. R. D. 32, 79
Leale Ltd 41, 50, 83
leather cutters 32
leather merchants 39
Le Bailliage (newspaper) 84
Le Carpentier, Mr. A. 49
Le Cheminant, Miss 45, 50
Le Cheminant, Mr. 32, 46, 50
Le Cheminant, Mr. A. 27, 72
Le Cheminant, Mr. F. 28
Le Cheminant, Mr. John 32, 66
Le Cocq, Mr. Amice 38
lectures 64
Le Duc, Mrs. Oliver 31
Lee, Rev. G.E. 34
Lefebvre Street 70, 83
Le Grand Carrefour 15, 21
Le Huray, Mrs. 27
Le Lacheur, Mr. 20, 43
Le Lacheur, Mr. E. 20
Le Lacheur, Mrs 13
Le Lièvre, Mrs. 27, 83
Le Marchant Street 53

Le Noury, Mr. and Mrs. 44
Le Noury, Mrs. 27, 42
Le Page, Messrs P & Son 14
Le Page, Miss 38
Le Page, Mr. jun 14
Le Patourel, Mr. 19, 83
Le Pelley, Miss 51
Le Pelley's Field 56
Le Petit Carrefour 33, 38, 41
Lequilbecq, Mr. 40
Lequilbecq, Mr. F. 40
Lequilbecq, Mr. Victor 40
Le Riche 17, 21
Le Riche's Stores 5, 40
Les Côtils 59
Les Croûtes 71
Les Gravées 40, 55, 59, 75
Les Gravées du Sud 55
Les Hubits 74
Les Préaux, St Martin's 75
Les Rocquettes 55
L'Etacq 86
Le Tissier, Mr. 51
Le Vallon (house) 59
Le Vrangue 74
Le Vrangue Mill 20, 74
L'Hyvreuse 59
Libraries
    Candie Library 60
    Guille-Allès Library 30, 32, 33, 64
    Priaulx Library. *See* Candie Library
lifebuoys 80
Lighthouse, Hanois 76
Lihou, Captain 87
Lihou, Mr. 27, 43, 45
Livermore Bros' Minstrels 65
Livery Stables 71
Lloyd's Bank 21
Loaring, Mr. C. 43
lobsters 37, 92
lobster shells 72
Lock and Son, Messrs. 74
Lombardy House 38
London 19, 75, 76, 85, 87
London and Midland Bank 19
London Brewery 75
London House 19
London Queen (ship) 85
London & South-Western Railway Co. 85
Lovell and Co. Ltd 49

Lovell and Cox, Messrs. 48, 49
Lovell, Mr. sen. 49
Lower Pollet 23
Luce, Miss 44
Luff & Co. 44, 45
Luff, Mr. W. 40, 46, 77
Lukis House 54
Lydia (ship) 89
Lynx (ship) 90

M

MacCulloch, Sir Edgar 23, 33
MacGregor, Mr. 55
MacGregor, Mr. A. 59
Machon, Mrs. 5, 23
Mackay, Messrs and Co 27
Mackenzie, Mr. 83
Maguire, Mr. 74
Mahaut, Alphonse 24
Mahy, Mr. 37
Mail and Telegraph (newspaper) 82, 83
mailboat 66, 89
Maillard, Mr. 79, 83
Mainguy, General 55
Maison Blicq 39, 73
Maison Carré 27
Maison Cohu 17
Manger, Mr. A. E. 77
Manor Place 71, 84
Mansell, Alfred 20
Mansell Court 44, 45
Mansell, Mr. Jno. 59
Mansell Street 40, 43, 45, 46, 50
Manuelle's quarry 81
Marie, Mons. Jean 40
Maritime Inn (public house) 31
Market Hotel 32, 54
Markets 27–31
Market Square 26, 33
Market Steps 29, 30
Market Street 27, 32, 51
Marmain's Stores 8, 45, 46
Marmion, Rev. R. Walton 59
Marquand, Alfred 20
Marquand, Mr. 40
Marquand, Mr. David 29
Marquand, Mr. J.B. 20
Marquand, Mr. W. 44
Marquis, Mr. 49

martello tower 81
Martel, Mr. N. 40
Martel, Mrs. 32
Martel, Mr. Thomas jun. 91
Martin Bros 46, 91
Martin, Capt. Abm. 91
Martin, Mme. 40
Martin, Mr. 33, 60
Martin, Mr. Stephen 60
Mary Ann (ship) 93
Massart, Mrs. 45
Masters, Miss 43
Masters, Mr. R. 40
Masters's Yard 40
Mauger, Mr. 34, 79
Mauger, Mr. H. de Jersey 60
Mauger, Mr. Mansell 32
Maunder, Mr. 24
Maxwell brothers 77
Maxwell, Mrs. 77
May (boat) 65, 91
McAdam 11
McCrea, Colonel and Mrs. 59
Meat Market 31, 32, 33
Mechanics' Institute 33
medical practitioners 23
Mellish, Mr. C. 33
Mellish, Mr. T. 33
Melrose (house) 55, 59
Military
    barracks 80
    garrison 66, 80
    regimental bands 63, 65
    soldiers 80
Militia. *See* Royal Guernsey Militia
Miller, Mr. Wm. 71, 72
milliners 21, 27, 28, 29, 43, 46, 50
Millington, Mr (bookshop) 20
Mill Street 41, 42–44, 73, 84
mineral waters 40
Molesworth, Hon. 43
monks, community in Herm 77
Monro, Messrs. G. and Co. 92
Moon, Mr. H. 41
Moon (newspaper) 84
Mordacque, Misses 59
Morlaix, Brittany 86
Morning Herald (newspaper) 84
Morning Star (ship) 93
motorists 55

Mould, Mr. 33
Moulin Huet 74
Moulin Huet Mill 20, 74
Mrs. Amy's School 37
Murdoch, Mr. 32
Murdoch, Mr. W. D. 40, 46
Murdoch's Store 32
Museum 33
music shop 69
Myers, Mr. 30

N

Naftel, Mr. 33
Naftel, Paul 33
National and Provincial Bank 20
Nelson Place 14
Neve, Mrs. 54, 55
Newbury, Messrs. W. and 77
Newbury, Mr. 50
newsagents 49
newspapers 83–84
New Street 53, 83
New Town 11
Nicolle, Mr. 19
Nicolle, Mrs. 33, 41
Nicolle's 38
Nightingale, Mr. sen. 72
Nightingale, Two-Headed 65
Non Pareil (boat) 91
Norfolk House 54
Normandy (ship) 85
Norton Bavant, Wiltshire 20
Norton, Mr. G. H. 71
Norton, Mr. H. 71
Nutt, Commodore 64

O

oak, Grecian 76
Oates, Rev. J. 59
Œnone (ship) 86
Ogier, Mr. 19
Old Bank 20, 90
olive oil 44
Ollivier, Misses 28
Ollivier, Mr. 40
onion sellers 86
organists 17
Orme, Col. 77

Osborne, Messrs. 30
Osmington (house) 92
ouaie sauvage. *See* wild goose
Ozanne and Aubert 50
Ozanne and Haysom 46
Ozanne, Mr. 49
Ozanne, Mrs. 46
Ozanne, Rev. R. J. 59
Ozanne's Mill 20, 74

P

paddle steamer 85, 86, 87, 93
Paen, Mr. 27
Paint, Mr. 27, 28
Palmer, Mr. "Nellie" 72
paperhangers 14, 43
Parade Field 65
Paradis (house) 55
Parish Church, St Peter Port 17, 34, 59
Park Street 24
Parry, Miss 17
Parry, Misses 19
Parsons, J. H. 30
pastrycooks 17, 28, 41
Patois. *See* Guernésiais
Paul, Mr. E. 40
pawnshops 38
Payne, Mr. 44, 60
Pearse, Mrs. 92
Pedvin Street 51, 77
Pengelley, Mr. 32, 51
Perchard's Stables 55
perfumery 21
Perkins, Rev. 59
Perrot, Mons. Y. 49
Petherick, Mrs. 43
Petit Bot 9, 74
Petit Bot Mill 20, 74
Petit Carrefour 41
Petitt, Mr. 49
pharmacy 23
Philharmonic Concerts 64
Phillips, Miss S. M. 46
photographers 13, 23, 30, 38, 51, 53
piano dealers 15, 17, 19
pianoforte professor 75
Picquet House 34
Pierce, Mrs. 92
Piprell, Captain 86

Plantation 53, 55
Platte Boue 89
playwrights 64
plumbers 44
Plymouth, Devon 85
Plymouth (ship) 85
Poids de la Reine 31
Police Force 60
Police Station 53
Pollet 22–25
Portinfer Bay 76
Postmaster 29
postmen 39
Post Office 14, 28
poulterers 30, 31, 86
Priaulx Library 8. *See also* Candie Library
Prima Donna (boat) 91
Prince of Wales' House 17, 21
Princess (ship) 86, 91
printers 84
publicans 34
Pulias 76
pumps 39, 40, 69

Q

Quarry, Manuelle's 81
Quay Street 11
Queen of the Isles (ship) 86
Queen's Birthday 65
Queen's Hotel 54
Queen's Road 59, 71
Queen Victoria 59
Quesnel, Captain 86
Quick, Mr. A.C. 34

R

radio engineers 29
Ralls, Mr. 49
Ralls, Mr. sen. 49
Randall, Mr. R. H. 66
Randell and Son, Messrs. 51
Randell, Mr. J. B. 33, 66
Randell, Mr. sen. 51
Ray, Mr. 32, 43
Ray, Mr. sen. 32
rectors 34, 59
Rectory House 30, 31, 33
refreshment rooms 92

Reindeer (ship) 86
Renier, Mr. 43
Renouf, Mr. 50, 74
Renouf, Mr. J. W. 49
Rescue (boat) 87, 88
Rescue II (boat) 87, 88
restaurants 27, 29, 44
Reynolds (née Digard), Mrs. J.J. 19
Richmond Avenue 56
Richmond Corner 81
Ridgway, Advocate 83
Ridout's Nursery 54
Riskey, Miss 15
Robert, Mr. 39
Robert, Mr. Ernest 39
Roberts, Dr. 53, 59
Roberts, Mr. 71
Robin, Miss Gallienne 18
Robin, Mr. 19, 28, 32, 37
Robin, Mr. Amice 38
Robin, Mr. Fred. 93
Robin, Mr. Thos. 43
Robinson, Dr. E.L. 77
Roger, Mr. A. P. 5, 23, 28
Rohais 20, 56, 77
roller skating. *See* skating
Rope Walk, St. John's 74
Rosaire Avenue 55
Rosemary Lane 37
Roseneath (house) 59
Rouge Huis Avenue 54
Rouge Huis (house) 55
Rouge Rue 74
Rougier, Mr. 19, 37
Rousby, Mr. Wybert 64
Roussel, Mr. Peter 17
Rowe, Mr. senr. 27
Rowley, Mr. 63
Royal Guernsey Militia 64, 65, 66
    officers 66
        Rifle Regiment 65
    service 66
Royal Hotel 52, 54
Rue A l'Or 69
Rue Marguerite 53
Ruettes Brayes 59, 73

S

saddlers 33, 34, 40

sailors 40, 80
Salem Chapel 50
Salerie 81
Salter Street 53
salt stores 40
Salvation Army 64
sand-eeling 63
Sark 6, 59, 63, 87, 88
Sarnia Fruit Co. 23
Sarre, Mr. 60
Satterley, Mr. 37
Saunders, J.S. 47
Sausmarez windmill 20, 74
Scandinav (ship) 88
schoolchildren 30, 65
Schools
    Boys' Secondary School 77
    Elizabeth College 37
    Mrs. Amy's School 39
scissors grinders 70
Scotland 81
Scott, Captain 86
sea captains 18, 93
Seawitch of London (ship) 76
Sebire, Mrs. 31, 32
Secondary School, Boys' 37
secondhand goods 40
seedsman 49
Seigneur of Sark 59, 87. *See also* Collings,
    Rev. W.
Senner, Messrs. 50
Sharp, Mr. 77
Sharshaw, Mrs 23
Shaw, Mr. J 14
Shayer, Mr. 45, 50
Shayer, Mr. jun. 45
sheep 54, 73
Sheppard, Dr. 41
Sheppard, Mr. 50
Sheriff 60, 79
Sheriff, Mr. 33
shipbuilding
    blocks 74
    lengthening 90
    ropewalk 74
    sailmakers 74
    sawyers 74
    shipyard 53
Shipping
    catering 90

life rafts 89
rowing boats 91
sailing and steam yachts 92
sailing boats 90, 91
sailing ships 90, 93
schooners 86
screw-steamers 85, 86, 87, 89
security for passengers 89
steamers 19, 85, 86, 87, 89, 90, 93
yachts 92
ships 19, 85–93
shipwrecks 76, 86, 89
Shirvell, Mr. 50, 54
shoeshops 17, 28, 40, 74
shooting 76
Sierra Leone 76
signwriters 83
silk mercers 19
Simmonds, Mr. 77
singers, comic 64
Sir William Place 23
skating rink 63
Smithard, Mr. H. 72
Smith, Mr. 29
smiths, shoeing 51
smiths, tin 23, 40
Smith Street 5, 12–15, 43
smiths, white 50
Sneath, Mr. 83
Society of Natural Science 77
Solent 85
Southampton (ship) 85, 89
South-Western Railway Co. 89, 92, 93
South-Western (ship) 89
spelling bees 64
Spencer, Mr. R. L. 85
Spiller, Mr. Levi 32
Spong, Mr. 30
Staddon, Mrs. 28
Stafford, Mr. 39
St. Andrew's 57
Stanley Road 56
Stannington (ship) 85
Staperayder (ship) 85, 86
Star, The (newspaper) 7, 8, 27, 41, 82, 83,
    84
States Arcade 31
States' Electric Showroom 20
States' Offices 38
States officials 91

States of Guernsey 81
States' Savings Bank 17, 38
St. Brieuc, Brittany 86
Stedman, Mr. 37, 81
Stella (ship) 89
St. George Street 51
Stickland, Mr. 86
Stickland's (bookshop) 21
St. James's Church 59
St. James's Place 53, 59
St. James's Street 53
St. Johns 74
St. John's Ambulance 77
St. John's Church 59
St. John's Home for Orphans 77
St. John Street 71
St. Joseph's Church 7, 59
St. Julian's Avenue 5, 52, 53, 69
St. Julian's Hall 64, 65
St. Malo, Brittany 86
St. Martin's 75, 93
stone trade 11, 13, 74, 79, 87, 92
    Manuelle's quarry 81
    stone cracking 74
    stone dressing 74
St. Peter-in-the-Wood Church 59
Street, Mr. James 23
Stribley, Mrs. 29
Stroobant, Mr. 34, 44
St. Sampson's 81, 87, 93
St. Sampson's Church 59
St. Sampson's Harbour 87
Summerland (house) 75
Swaffield, Mr. 32
Swallow (boat) 91
Swanage, Dorset 51
Sylf (boat) 91
Symes, Mr. 43, 44
Symth3on, Mr. 30

Taylor, Mr. 50
tea merchants 13, 30
Telegraph Office 34
telephones, public 56
Thackrey, Mr. 49
theatre, near Court House 64
Theatre Royal 53
The Times (newspaper) 69
Thomas, Mrs 15
Thoumine, Mr. 60
Thumb, General Tom 64
tip-smiths 45
tobacconists 19, 20, 29, 32, 39, 41, 44, 45,
    46, 49, 50, 60, 92
Toms, Mr. 84
Torode and Nicolle 41
Torode, Messrs 19
Torode, Mr. J.B. 14, 33
Tower Hill 40
Town Church 35. *See* Parish Church, St
    Peter Port
Town Crier 70
Town Mills 24
toyshops 13, 17, 20, 28, 41, 43, 45, 72
tramway 75, 80, 81
Trinity Square 48–49
Trouteaud, Mr. 38
Truchot 23, 53
Trump, Mr. 70
Tucker, Mr. 32
Tudor House 39, 46
tugs 87, 88
Tupper, Jurat Col. de Vic 59
Turner, Mr. H. 15, 42, 43, 73
Turner, Mr. T. 17, 24
turners 50, 74
Two-Headed Nightingale (conjoined twins)
    65
Tyler's (shop) 17

T

tailors 19, 32, 37, 46
Talbot, Mr. 83
talent, local histrionic 64
Tardif, Mr. 20, 92
Targett and Hicks, Messrs. 51
Taudevin, Mr. 72
Taudevin, Mr. S. 85, 93
taxidermist 27

U

umbrellas 13, 33, 45, 86
upholsterers 49
Upland Road 51
Upper Mansell Street 49
urchins 60
Utermarck, J. de H. 50
Utermarck, Mr. 60

V

Vale Church 59
Valnord Bank 56
Valpied, Mr. 19
Valpy and Son, Messrs. 49
Vancour, Charles 20
Varna House 56, 57
Vauvert 44, 49–50, 72, 74
Vauvert Hardware Co. 50
Vegetable Market 29, 33
vegetables 31, 33
velocipede 24, 70
Ventnor (house) 56
Verdala (house) 56
Verinder, Mr. 19
veterinary surgeon 75
Victoria Crescent 23
Victoria Hotel 54
Victoria House 18, 19
Victoria, Queen 59
Victoria Road 23, 32, 44, 49, 55
Victoria Tower 55
Vincent, Miss 27
Vincent, Mr. 33
vingteniers 66
Violet Villa 50
visitors 63, 72

W

wages, servants' 74
waggonettes 71
Wallis, Mr. 43
Wardley, Mr. 31
Warren, Miss Minnie 64
Warr, Mr. 40
Washington, Mr. 93
watchmakers 14, 21, 32, 38, 43
Waterloo House 20, 32
Waterman, Mr. 23
Waverley (ship) 85, 89
wayfarers 79
Way, Messrs. and Sons 43
Webber, Mr. 37, 44
Webber, Mr. B. 40
Weeks, Mrs. 32
Wellman, Colonel 59
Westever, Mr. E.N. 20
Westminster Bank 20

Weymouth, Dorset 63, 85, 90, 93
Weysom, Mr. F. J. 37
Wheadon, Mr. G. 38
Wheadon, Mrs. 15
Wheadon, Mrs. G. 13, 51
Wheadon, Mr. T. H. 29
wheelwrights 54, 55
Whicker, Mr. 40, 43
Whinfield, Mr. Paul 14
Whitehead, Mr. 38
White, Miss C. 41
wild goose. *See* goose, wild
Williams, Mr. 60, 91
Wimbledon 66
wine and spirit merchants 21, 23, 24, 27,
    38, 40, 49
wines and spirits 92
wireless dealers 44
Working Men's Association 23, 64
Wyatt's, Messrs. 24

Y

Yacht Hotel 54
York Avenue 56
Young, Mr. T. 51

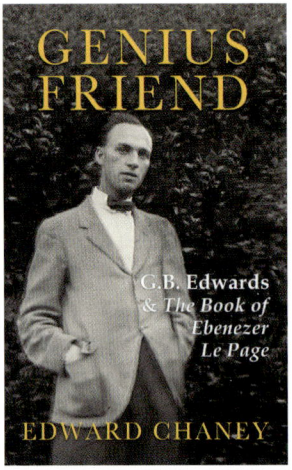

**Genius Friend:
G.B. Edwards and The Book
of Ebenezer Le Page**

Edward Chaney

ISBN 978-0992879105
Published: September 2015
Blue Ormer Publishing
Price: £19.99

Since its publication in 1981, *The Book of Ebenezer Le Page* has been recognised as the greatest work of literature by a native Guernseyman, and indeed one of the greatest novels of the twentieth century.

Edward Chaney befriended its reclusive author, Gerald Edwards, encouraged him to finish the novel and had it published after he bequeathed him the manuscript. This two-part biography reconstructs Gerald's Guernsey origins and his status as the 'genius friend' of a group of writers who contributed to Middleton Murry's *Adelphi* in the 1920s. It then documents his descent into obscurity in the 1940s. The second part relates how Chaney met Edwards in Dorset in 1972 and how the novel eventually came to be published and was enthusiastically received.

'A consistently fascinating attempt to chart the life of a geniune literary outsider', D.J. Taylor, *Times Literary Supplement*

'... the author's researches and his personal knowledge of Edwards do bring this strange and wayward man to life.' William Palmer, *Literary Review*